THE
Unbelievable
TRUTH

A MEDIUM'S GUIDE
TO THE SPIRIT WORLD

GORDON SMITH

HAY HOUSE, INC.
Carlsbad, California
London • Sydney • Johannesburg
Vancouver • Hong Kong

Published and distributed in the United States by: Hay House, Inc., P.O. Box 5100, Carlsbad, CA 92018-5100 • *Phone:* (760) 431-7695 or (800) 654-5126 • *Fax:* (760) 431-6948 or (800) 650-5115 • www.hayhouse.com • **Published and distributed in Australia by:** Hay House Australia Pty. Ltd., 18/36 Ralph St., Alexandria NSW 2015 • *Phone:* 612-9669-4299 • *Fax:* 612-9669-4144 • www.hayhouse.com.au • **Published and distributed in the United Kingdom by:** Hay House UK, Ltd. • Unit 62, Canalot Studios • 222 Kensal Rd., London W10 5BN • *Phone:* 44-20-8962-1230 • *Fax:* 44-20-8962-1239 • www.hayhouse.co.uk • **Published and distributed in the Republic of South Africa by:** Hay House SA (Pty), Ltd., P.O. Box 990, Witkoppen 2068 • *Phone/Fax:* 27-11-706-6612 • orders@psdprom.co.za • **Distributed in Canada by:** Raincoast • 9050 Shaughnessy St., Vancouver, B.C. V6P 6E5 • *Phone:* (604) 323-7100 • *Fax:* (604) 323-2600

Editorial supervision: Jill Kramer   *Design:* Summer McStravick

Library of Congress Cataloging-in-Publication Data

Smith, Gordon, 1962-
  The unbelievable truth : a medium's guide to the spirit world / Gordon Smith.
    p. cm.
  Includes bibliographical references.
  ISBN 1-4019-0358-4 (hardcover) — ISBN 1-4019-0362-2 (tradepaper) 1. Parapsychology. I. Title.
  BF1031.S625 2004
  130--dc22

2004014838

ISBN 13: 978-1-4019-0362-6
ISBN 10: 1-4019-0362-2

07 06 05 04   5 4 3 2

1st printing, September 2004
2nd printing, August 2005

Printed in the United States of America

FOR MY MOTHER, MY FATHER, AND MY FAMILY . . .

AND ALL THOSE WHO HAVE INSPIRED ME.

Contents

It never ceases to amaze me how many people have questions about "the unexplained"—questions about ghosts and miracles, reincarnation, life after death, and out-of-body and near-death experiences. Subjects like these and many more have fascinated me since childhood. Ever since I was very young, I've seen the spirits of people who have died. I had my first-ever paranormal experience when I saw the spirit of someone close to our family shortly after his death, and my mother's reaction was one of shock and horror. She forbade me from ever mentioning my encounters with spirit people . . . yet later on, I still managed to become a recognized medium.

Mediums have been providing evidence of spirit survival for many years, but that's just the first step in investigating the unseen world around us. Most people have encountered something strange at some point in their lives, which made them look differently at the world they live in. Some have witnessed spirits who appeared to give warnings or messages to their loved ones; while others have heard children give accurate accounts of previous lives, have experienced miraculous healings, or seen spirits or angels. One of the biggest questions I was left with when putting together some of the amazing stories in this book was why, if so many individuals have experienced so many supernatural occurrences, don't we hear more about them?

One reason, I believe, is that there are so many myths and mysteries attached to the paranormal that many people don't know what to believe. I can understand this—after all, I've been around the world of psychics, mediums, and all sorts of so-called spiritual practitioners for much of my life, and I've personally experienced some amazing phenomena. But even so, I certainly don't believe everything I've been exposed to, and neither would I expect others to. Not everyone who claims to be psychic actually is, so it's important to learn to see past the charade and find the truth—whatever that may be.

In *The Unbelievable Truth,* I've attempted to shed some light on the dark corners of life: the places where ignorance can breed fear. I've spent most of my life trying to convince people that there indeed is life after death, yet the mediumship I share is only one small part of the bigger picture of our continued life. Once we accept that our spirit will live on after death, then this inevitable question follows: What is it like in the afterlife? And *where* is the afterlife? Where do we go? Is there a heaven and hell, and what qualifies you to go to one or the other?

What I've found is that to understand anything about the nature of the unseen world, we first have to try to understand our own nature—that is, to become conscious of who we are, where we've come from, and where we're going. It's in the learning about ourselves and our consciousness that we can overcome our fears and doubts and accept what once seemed beyond belief as normal, everyday, and even reassuring. And then, all of a sudden, we'll realize that life is playing out as it should.

I've been directly involved with many of the episodes in this book, while others have been shared with me by those who have encountered unbelievable happenings and have allowed me to investigate them further. Many of these accounts may appear to be unbelievable, but I can assure you that they're all actually the truth (to the best of my knowledge).

Writing this book has been one of the most enlightening journeys I've made on my spiritual path. I hope that you'll enjoy reading it as much as I did writing it, but more than that, I sincerely hope that it helps you in your own search for truth.

Chapter One

MEDIUMS AND PSYCHICS

What does it mean to be a medium? Well, it isn't always easy to explain what I actually do. Saying that I communicate with discarnate spirits who have gone on after physical death sounds strange to some people. They'll ask me, "What sort of messages are passed on? And what convinces people that their loved ones are really communicating with them?" I've often thought that a good way to explain the process would be to film someone before they came to see me and ask them to share their story and what they hoped to gain from the encounter.

In January 2004 that very thing happened during the filming of a BBC documentary in which a couple who had lost their son in a car accident the

1

year before was brought to see me. Unbeknownst to me, the couple had actually been filmed for some time before our meeting. In fact, the director of the film hadn't allowed me to have any prior knowledge of the couple at all, not even where they were being brought from. (This should actually be standard practice, as the less the medium knows about a person, the more convincing the evidence they may receive from the spirit world.)

On a cold February morning, I was waiting in the library of the London Spiritual Mission, where the sitting was to take place. This is one of the most beautiful Spiritualist churches in the United Kingdom, where mediums from all over the country come to demonstrate their skills. Once the film crew decided that they were ready to begin, a couple whom I guessed were in their 40s was asked to sit down opposite me. I explained to them how the sitting would proceed.

Now, I normally "tune in" to the spirit world by asking the spirit people if they'd like to come and contact their loved ones, but this time, even as I began to tell the couple how the process might work, I could hear the voice of a young man shouting the name "Andrew" over and over in my ear. With this, I knew that I had a communicator from the spirit world, so I started by saying, "There's a young man on the Other Side, and he's asking for Andrew."

Immediately, the man answered, "I'm Andrew."

Then I heard another name, so I turned to the woman and said, "You must be Margareta."

"No," she answered.

"I'm sorry," I replied, "he's changed it to Greta." This time, the woman smiled and confirmed that that was her name.

Their son was now communicating at high speed, often so fast that I had to slow him down—which his mother said was characteristic of how he'd behaved in life. The spirit told me that his name was Nige, short for Nigel, and that he and his friend were together in the spirit world, as they'd both been involved in the same accident. He went on to ask after other family members, told me to tell his sister to go back to school, and mentioned a Mr. Trainer, who turned out to be her tutor at college. Then he asked me to mention a place called Ilkley, where he'd been brought up and had spent much of his time with his teenage friends.

Nige wanted to convince his family that he was still very much a part of their life, so he beseeched me to ask his father why no one was wearing his watch, which was at home in a blue box. His father said that he wanted to, but hadn't gotten around to putting in the new battery that it needed. Then Nige told his mother that he'd been with her that morning when she'd picked up three letters from behind the front door. He also knew that she'd wanted to bring the large picture of him with her to the sitting [another name for a reading], but instead she'd picked it up, touched his face, and put it back. He also said that she could feel his presence when she walked through the lane at the back of her house. All of this was accepted by Andrew and Greta.

Nige then asked me to tell them that he'd been with them when they'd gone to Ilkley Moor and stood on his favorite large rock. The camera operators and soundmen were shocked at this, as they'd filmed the family walking on Ilkley Moor the previous day—when Andrew had stood on his son's favorite rock and said that Nige would say that it was like standing on top of the world. At the close of the sitting, the crew again got a bit spooked when young Nige asked me to tell them all that he and his friend were fine and that he really was standing on top of the world.

Afterward, Greta and Andrew told me how moved and uplifted they'd been by the sitting. They felt that their son's personality had truly shone through, and their overwhelming impression had been that he really was communicating with them. They were absolutely amazed that Nige's spirit had been with them when they'd been filmed on the moors, and that he'd then been able to tell them about it through my mediumship.

An encounter like this may be able to provide people with enough evidence to convince them that their loved ones live on after death, and thus help heal their grief. As a medium, my main task is to help those who need to find hope and comfort at such times.

DELIVERING MESSAGES . . .

One of the greatest mediums of the last century was my old friend Albert Best. So detailed were his messages that people would often appear bewildered by his knowledge of their loved ones' lives. He'd talk to the unseen, receive answers as though it were all quite normal, and would often tell me about his experiences, including private sittings with celebrities and politicians from all over the world.

There are so many unbelievable episodes of mediumship associated with Albert, but one stands out in my mind because of who the person involved was.

❀ ❀ ❀

Rev. David Kennedy, a Church of Scotland minister, was sitting with his wife, Ann, as she lay dying in a hospital bed in Glasgow. She was only in her 40s, but David knew that there was no cure for her illness and that she'd be gone in a very short time. So frail was her body that he couldn't even hold her close to him, but so brave was her spirit that she reassured him that she'd find a way to come back to him from beyond the grave. And even though it was against his religious belief, he agreed to look for a sign from her.

The death of his wife hit David extremely hard. He found life increasingly difficult without her, and his faith in God was being tested to its very limits. Remembering her vow to give him a sign that her spirit lived on, he went to visit Spiritualist medium Lexie Findletter, who gave him a message from a woman named Ann who claimed to be his wife. David's natural skepticism and religious conditioning wouldn't allow him to accept this message; nevertheless, as he got up to leave the room, Mrs. Findletter said, "Your wife is determined to communicate with you, and she will find a way."

A week after his meeting with the medium, David felt even worse. Had his wife really been trying to get a message through to him? What if he hadn't given her a proper chance? In despair, he cried out to the empty room, "Come on, Ann, give me a sign, something that no one could possibly know. Please!"

He lay down on the sofa, feeling exhausted at the thought of the sermon he'd have to prepare for his service later that day. The next thing he knew, he was awakened by the sound of the phone ringing. Lifting his head from the arm of the sofa, he looked at the clock on the wall and started to panic, as he realized that he only had five minutes to prepare his sermon and find a clean minister's collar. Ignoring the phone, he fumbled around the room looking for old notes and trying to remember where his clean collars were. Still the phone rang. David grabbed the receiver and angrily barked, "Can I help you?"

"Your wife, Ann, is with me," said a voice. "She tells me that your clean collars are in the bottom drawer of your wardrobe, and the speech you prepared last year for this service is in the top drawer of your desk. Incidentally, my name is Albert Best. Good-bye."

David was stunned as he remembered that he and his wife had met Albert some years before at a social gathering. People had been raving about his skills as a medium, when from out of the blue, Albert had told Ann that her brother, who had died during World War II, was standing beside her—and then he proceeded to give a perfect description of him. But how did Albert Best know to phone at that moment with the exact information David needed? And how did he get the number?

The reverend went about his business as best he could that evening, but in the weeks that followed, he set about finding Albert and putting his powers to the test. He found out that Ann had appeared to the medium in spirit form and had provided the information about the collars and the sermon, as well as the phone number. As time passed, David learned that if he sent out a thought to his wife when he was alone in the house, within a short time Albert would be on the phone with the answer. Once he even said, "Tell your bloody wife to stop bloomin' bothering me—it's the middle of the night!" And so it was: David had forgotten how late it was when he'd sent the thought to Ann, and now it was past 3 A.M.!

This continued for more than a year. I remember Albert telling me that he'd often get annoyed with Ann's frequent requests for him to call her husband. But the more he protested, the more strongly the visions of Ann appeared, and the more clearly she spoke to him. Albert knew that she felt she had some kind of mission to convince her husband of her survival, and it was obvious that she was going to stay on his case until her work was done.

Messages from the Other Side certainly weren't part of David Kennedy's own religious teaching, but the more he tried to reason them away, the more baffled he became. Finally, he asked Ann to do one more thing to prove her survival—and he told her that this time he would accept it. He asked her to give him a message through Albert concerning something about herself of which he knew nothing, and then to confirm it through a member of her own family. The next time Ann appeared to Albert, she simply asked him if he'd tell her husband to call her sister and ask about the ballet shoes. When David did so, his sister-in-law was astounded that he knew of the private joke that had been a secret between her and Ann for many years.

This message finally convinced David, who was left with no choice but to accept that his wife's consciousness was still able to communicate with him after her physical death. What was also apparent was that in her new state, she was aware of his thoughts and actions and would respond to them through a medium. Most people don't realize that when they send out a thought, it might very well be picked up and often answered by someone on the Other Side. In this case, it was certainly clear that Ann's spirit was receiving all her husband's messages, but David needed help to pick up the ones she sent back. So using a medium ultimately enabled him to get over his loss and get on with his life, comforted by the knowledge that Ann's consciousness had survived. To me, this is the reason why mediums are given such a gift.

After much thought and investigation into his experiences, David Kennedy decided to write his story, which later became a book called *A Venture into Immortality*. (Incidentally, Albert Best worked as a mail carrier for most of his life—delivering messages is what he was good at!)

TRUTHS AND MISCONCEPTIONS ABOUT MEDIUMS

There are so many misconceptions about mediums, that as a working medium myself, I feel it's my duty to reveal the truth about what mediums can't, don't, or even won't do!

Myth #1: Mediums call up the dead.
On the contrary—spirit people attract the attention of the particular medium they feel attuned to in order to contact their loved ones.

Myth #2: Mediums go into weird trances, speak in funny accents, and know the answers to every mystery from why Atlantis sank to why British tennis players are so bad.
The truth is . . . no, they don't.

Myth #3: Mediums are always overweight, postmenopausal women or youngish gay men.
No, they come in all shapes and sizes.

Myth #4: Mediums always have Native American spirit guides.
There *are* lots of Native American guides, but they're probably only there to try to sort out some of the cowboys who call them-selves mediums.

Myth #5: All mediums use crystal balls to look into the future.

A crystal ball is a psychic prop similar to tarot cards and rune stones. A medium should be able to make contact with the spirit world without the aid of such props.

Myth #6: Mediums can call up anyone you might want to talk to on the Other Side.

The truth is that we mediums can't demand to make contact with a particular spirit. For example, if fans of Elvis Presley went to a medium and wanted to make contact with their hero, the chances are that nothing much would happen. If, however, Mr. Presley's daughter went for a sitting, then there would be a spiritual link between the two of them, so maybe he would communicate with her. (But what am I thinking? Isn't Elvis still alive?!)

MEDIUMS AND PSYCHICS

Many people seem to associate mediums with those psychics who consult crystal balls or tarot cards. The sad thing is, they couldn't be further from the truth. While all mediums are psychic, not all psychics are mediums.

You see, people who are psychic exhibit many different skills, including the ability to pick up information about someone's past, present, and even future. Some of them can move objects using the power of their mind, others can read thoughts, and still others can heal the sick. All of these phenomena and more come under the *psychic* banner because they're produced from a person's own psychic energy field, not from the spirit world.

Some psychics have used their powers in very positive ways: They've assisted the police with murder cases by using psychometry to tune in to an object or piece of clothing taken from a crime scene, and have given detailed information about the particular crime, often with great success; while others have just helped detectives with their inquiries. It's also been said that psychics were used by the military during the Cold War as remote viewers. (*Remote viewing* is when a person uses his or her mind to see events at a great distance.)

Someone with true psychic awareness can certainly access notable events in a person's life just by looking at him or her. Normally, these are events that are stored in the emotional "databases" of the mind—the psychic picks up on the emotional turbulence and uses it to establish a link to the person's mind. Once they have such a link, they can usually come up with what's currently giving him or her problems, and can then offer guidance.

Fake Psychics

A good psychic may help you through a difficult time in your life, but like all things of this nature, there *are* charlatans among us. It's all too easy to find a problem, offer a solution, and maybe polish the ego along the way. Who wouldn't feel better after that? Check the emotions and the body language—and throw in the usual generalities such as births, deaths, and marriages—and you have a successful reading. Cloud the memory with some psychobabble, using terms the clients have never heard before, then make them feel good before they leave. Then they'll rave to all of their friends about how good the reading was, if only because they've just been stung for $50 to $100 (or more).

It may be fun to invite a psychic into your home to read for a group of your friends, but do remember that he or she may do more harm than good. My watchwords are *common sense:* If you feel that the psychic is asking questions of you rather than making statements that are relevant to your life, then they're probably guessing.

I remember one poor man who came to see me after he'd lost his wife and had been visiting a lot of psychics in an effort to contact her on the Other Side. He'd found most of these people through advertisements in newspapers and magazines. All these con artists had charged him exorbitant amounts of money for their services, yet there hadn't been so much as a whisper from his dear wife. One woman told him that his gay partner in the spirit realms was trying to contact him, while another had given him a message from a great-aunt Fanny he didn't have. And most of these psychic practitioners claimed to be direct descendants of the famous Gypsy Rose Lee—what *was* the old girl doing in that tent to have so many direct descendants?

Sadly, between them, these "psychics" had taken so much money from this vulnerable man that he'd gone deep into debt and was pawning items from his home just to get by. That was bad enough, but by now he was so confused by everything he'd been told that he didn't know if he was coming or going. All I could do was try to bring some common sense back into his mind and steer him away from the psychic circus that trades on people in this state.

My old teacher in the Spiritualist church used to say of mediums and psychics who charged money for private sittings or readings that you could tell a good one by their price. By that she meant that the best were usually those who charged little or nothing for their gift.

Is There Anybody There?

Psychics make no claims to contact spirits on the Other Side, but many of them will stumble into situations where they begin to detect spirit messages in the space around their sitter. Yet even in this type of incident, they're not communicating directly with the discarnate spirit; instead, they're passing on information that the spirit has tried to convey to their loved one and that has remained in their *aura,* or electromagnetic field. Mediums, on the other hand, work from a stronger battery that boosts their signal farther afield, thus enabling them to pick up signals from the conscious minds of those who have gone on to the spirit world.

Although a medium's range reaches the spirit realms, it also covers the psychic-energy field, so a medium can also pick up information psychically from a person. Even though I'm a medium who gives messages from the spirit world, I very often sense what people close to me are thinking or feeling, and on many occasions, I can see images of future events in their lives. This happened to me often as a child, when my gift was more unrefined; it wasn't until I joined the development class in my local Spiritualist church that I began to understand the difference between my psychic abilities and my mediumship.

❀ ❀ ❀

A development class is made up of people wishing to develop their mediumistic or psychic abilities. Within the group or circle, there's a leader who will remain fully conscious and aware while the rest of the group still their minds and go within to a state of silence. This collection of people emitting psychic energy leads to a much stronger battery of power, and the energy around each sitter becomes very intense. The medium has to learn to focus his or her mind on this intense energy, as this is where the link with the spirit world is forged.

The best place to join one of these groups is a well-run Spiritualist church. The Spiritualist religion began more than 100 years ago and has grown to include hundreds of churches around Great Britain and in many countries around the world. In the early days, mediums produced many different types of phenomena in which the spirits not only communicated from the Other Side but would often materialize at séances. They could form in a physical way if the medium could produce a substance known as *ectoplasm,* which was often described as a "whitish, misty substance." Ectoplasm would be seen flowing out of the medium's body and would become dense enough to allow the spirits to mold it into their image. When fully materialized in this way, the spirits could walk freely around the people gathered, pick out their friends or relatives, and converse with them. This phenomenon was at its height in the Victorian era and throughout both world wars, when people were going to the Other Side *en masse*. Although many intelligent witnesses testified to having seen spirits materialize in this way, they were often criticized, because in order for the medium to produce ectoplasm, séances had to be held in the dark or in dim red light.

It would seem that with time, mediumship has refined and become more mental, in the sense that nowadays mediums hear, see, and sense spirit people rather than produce ectoplasm for them to materialize physically. Gone also are the days when Spiritualists would sit together, often around a large table, and hold hands while the leader or main medium would go into a trance in order to allow a highly evolved spirit to use his or her mind and body.

Spirit Guides

One thing that hasn't changed is that all mediums need to trust in a spirit guide or teacher. These are individuals who will make themselves known to you early in your development and who will guide each step you take on your spiritual journey. I consider this type of link between a medium and spirit guide to be like getting to know yourself on a higher level. Through the eyes of your guide, you can see the world in a much more compassionate and spiritual way.

Before I joined my development group, I'd never heard of spirit guides, even though I'd had experiences with spirit people since early childhood. But the idea that a teacher was going to give me lessons was interesting to say the least. "If I have a spirit guide, then what will they teach me?" I used to ask. "And anyway, why do I need one?"

The reason is that a spirit guide is like a safety point in your mind—an image, sense, or sound that allows you to journey through altered states of your own consciousness and beyond. Whenever things get to be too much or become too intense, you can call on your guide, in much the same way that children cry out for their parents when they feel lost.

Another valuable lesson I learned very early in this class was how to turn my gift on, and more important, how to switch it off. I feel very sorry for those who say that they have no control over this. If I couldn't switch off my mediumship, I dread to think what it would be like at the barbershop where I work. Can you imagine my asking a customer how he'd like his hair cut, only to hear his mother or father in the spirit world saying, "Cut it shorter—don't listen to him!"

The thing with spirit guides is that some people take the idea in completely the wrong way. There are those who begin to live the type of life they imagine the guide lived, and even worse, start to relate to the guide like a best friend. I remember one woman telling me that she had to change all the soft furnishings in her living room because her Tibetan guide stopped coming through to her when she had her curtains and cushions made from a Chinese fabric. Well, I never!

Many mediums claim to have well-known people as guides. In my early days in the development circle, I heard many "famous guides" channel through their new mediums. Along with many saints and legends such as Joan of Arc, John the Baptist, and so on, there would be the odd show-stopper such as Judy Garland, who came through a male medium and performed some of the more famous songs from her repertoire. I was also once told by the wife of a man who was developing trance mediumship that for several weeks her husband would get out of bed in the middle of the night wearing only his underpants, and talk in the voice of Elvis Presley for half an hour. His wife was so confused that she was "all shook up"! Another medium claimed that her guide was Beatles legend John Lennon. Can you *imagine?*

In my first three years in the development circle, most of my experiences were of the type of mental mediumship that I'd known from childhood, where I received messages in my mind. I'd also watched some mediums go into a trancelike state, and sometimes a different voice would speak through them. On certain occasions it would be like witnessing really bad acting, but there were a few times when the most astounding spiritual lectures would be given.

I always hoped that I'd personally never be involved in this type of mediumship. But then, one night I had the most amazing experience. I was sitting and trying to keep still, but as usual not a lot was happening and my mind started to drift. Then a light appeared in front of me, as if in the distance. Even though my eyes were shut tight, this light grew stronger, and eventually it was as if I were moving forward toward it. I felt illuminated and more alive than I ever had in my life, and then I seemed to fall asleep. Everything was peaceful, until I heard a voice that seemed to break the amazing silence. I immediately opened my eyes to see everyone in the group staring at me with looks of shock on their faces.

The leader of the group, Mrs. Primrose, moved closer to me and told me to take my time and come back slowly. As soon as she felt that I was fully awake, she asked me to join her in her office away from everyone else. I felt quite bewildered by all this, as all I'd done was fall asleep after having a marvelous experience. But Mrs. P. explained to me that my guide had spoken through me while I was in trance.

I was confused. "While I was in *what?!*"

She went on to say that the particular spirit teacher who works with me had given her a very specific message that she alone could understand and that might save a child's life in the not-too-distant future. When she finished talking, I was baffled—I had no knowledge of speaking, let alone of someone else speaking through me.

There was another occurrence of this "sleep-trance mediumship" one week later. This one also involved a child whose life was in danger, but miraculously she lived. To this day I have no memory of what was said through me, but I do know that the words came from someone who wanted to save a child's life, and I resolved that I'd try to find and trust whoever that was. I say "whoever" because mediums have more than one guide or teacher in the spirit world, so different ones may come through from time to time in accordance with the situation that needs their help. That particular spirit teacher, I've since come to learn, works with me whenever there's a need to help children. (It's a bit like having different doctors who specialize in their own field.)

Normally when I'm about to begin a private sitting for someone, I simply send out a thought to the spirit guides who help me, and within a second I become aware of who's helping me communicate with the spirit world. This is one of the skills I've learned to hone through years of meditation and the development of my awareness. Each spirit person who works with me has what I call their "calling card," or an indication of their identity that they "impress" upon me. For example, one who's very small in height will make me feel as if my body is shrinking, while another who has a beard will identify himself by making me aware of lots of facial hair, and so on.

Being able to recognize the spirit guides and helpers I've built up trust in over the years allows me to establish my first contact with the spirit world. It's through my guides that I proceed with questions on behalf of my sitter, such as "What was the person's name?" "When did they die?" or "How did they die?" During this process I may hear answers and pass them on to my sitter, or I may feel sensations of illness or infirmity that the spirit person lived through. Pictures may form in my mind of how the spirit person looked or of places where he or she lived or died. But most of what happens is sensed in feelings, which Spiritualists call *mental mediumship,* since they're of a subjective nature and occur within the mind of the medium.

GIVE WHAT YOU GET

When mediums have trust in their work, it boosts their signals to the spirit world. Also, trusting the spirit world is important because sometimes what comes through seems so trivial, yet it could mean so much to your sitter. An example of this happened to me recently, and it proved to me that as a medium, mine is not to reason why, but to simply give what I'm getting.

A lady in her mid-40s was sitting in the chair opposite me, and I was proceeding to give her the general rundown of how a private sitting should work, when I heard the voice of a young man by my left ear saying, "Mum, I'm here." I told the woman that she had a son in the spirit world, and he was communicating already. Soon I'd determined his name, how he passed away, and many features of his life. All seemed to be going well, until his mother asked me if I could ask him about the code that they'd come up with just before he died. I sent the thought out to her son, but nothing came back.

The woman's face fell, and I could tell that she'd lost all faith in what I was doing. I tried to explain that her son was trying to give as much information about himself as possible in the half hour that was allotted for his mother's sitting. I often look on a private sitting as the spirit person's chance to make a phone call. If you can imagine what you'd say to your family in what might be a one-time-only call, I'm sure it wouldn't be a very measured and concise conversation.

Finally, as the woman stood up to depart, I heard her son suddenly call out "Clover!" At this, she stared at me, shocked. Tears began to run down her cheeks, as she gasped, "Oh my God!" This was indeed the code that they'd agreed on. It turns out that when the boy was very young, he'd found a four-leaf clover for his mother while vacationing in England. In his late teens, he'd been diagnosed with cancer—and it was while he was in the hospital that the boy and his mother had agreed on the code that he'd use if he could communicate with her after death.

It's quite amazing to watch the reaction on someone's face when a certain piece of evidence comes through from the Other Side. Sometimes just a word or phrase can turn a light back on in a person's life. Usually it will be something simple, but so meaningful that they're moved from belief to knowing.

Science and Sensibility

A word or phrase may convince a relative, but what about scientists, who have been investigating mediumship for more than 100 years? During this time, scores of intelligent people have witnessed many forms of mediumship and have been convinced that paranormal phenomena were occurring right in front of them. But were they? With all forms of mediumship, for every genuine experience, there always seem to be a couple of charlatans just out to make money and prey on the vulnerable. (And I'm sure that back in the Victorian heyday of ectoplasm, the sale of muslin and cheesecloth went soaring up.)

In more recent times, I've allowed myself to be tested by the Scottish Society for Psychical Research, which is based at the University of Glasgow. Over the course of seven years or so, I've taken part in blind tests where I'm not permitted to see the recipients of my messages or hear their replies to anything I say. I've also taken part in what's called "double-blind tests," which involve my being asked to sit in one room while a group of people sits in another. One of these people is chosen by one of the scientists running the experiment, and I have to tune in to that person and give them a message (which they don't know they'll be receiving). At the end of the test, all the people present are given a sheet of paper with a list of the statements I've made, and they're asked to put a check next to any information that applies to them. And it usually turns out that the only person who can check all the boxes is the one who has been chosen to receive the message.

As part of other tests, I've had my head wired up to machines that register brain waves in order to determine my brain functions during a session of mediumship. Apparently my waves go from alpha to theta in around two minutes. I have no idea what to do with that knowledge, so I thought I'd just share it here!

I trained in my development group for approximately eight years, which is quite a long time for any apprenticeship. For the past 15 years, I've been practicing and demonstrating in private and public as a medium, and I find that the development of my mediumship continues as I learn from each person I meet. I've also discovered that if I use my gift to help those who are truly grieving, then, more often than not, there's a good result, and my sitter is uplifted by the experience. If, on the other hand, I were to use my psychic abilities just to impress people or make money, I'm sure that the results would be less than successful.

I've also learned through experience that if you seek help from mediums, you shouldn't go into the process with any preconceived ideas or expectations about what your loved one will tell you. It's best to remain open-minded and allow yourself to be given what you need, not what you think you want.

THE REASON WHY

More often than not, I'm asked, "Why do you do mediumship?" I frequently ask myself the same question, especially on a weekend when all my friends are going out while I head off to give a demonstration of my work.

This was precisely the case when I was working in my barbershop one day, feeling a bit down because a group of friends had invited me to a concert in Glasgow but I couldn't go because I was booked to work in a Spiritualist church in Edinburgh. The entire day I moped around, asking myself, "Why do I do mediumship?" The time seemed to drag, and the haircuts weren't looking too good, since I was becoming a bit heavy-handed with the electric clippers. Five o'clock did eventually arrive, so I prepared to close the salon. By now I was in a foul mood because all the staff had gone and I was left to tidy the shop.

I was still questioning the spirit world when my thoughts were interrupted by the sound of the door opening. Without thinking, I said loudly, "We're closed!"

Looking around, I saw a tall, well-built man in his 30s looking at me with a rather exasperated expression on his face. To cut a long story short, he wanted a shave, so I agreed to do it since I still had time to kill before going to the Spiritualist church.

As I applied the shaving cream, I had a strong impression of somebody watching me. The man was lying back in the barber's chair, face full of cream, quite relaxed by now, and saying nothing.

Holding my open razor to his throat, I began to shave him in silence, only to feel that same sensation of somebody watching me. I looked up at the mirror in front of me, and to my horror, I saw a young woman staring back at me.

I just didn't know how to react. *Who are you?* I thought.

"Judy," she replied at once. The impression was so strong that I knew she wanted me to speak to the man beneath my razor. Normally I'd never give messages to my clients, but this seemed so urgent that I had to.

"Do you know who Judy is?" I asked.

It was like an eruption—he sat bolt upright, almost joining the woman in the spirit world as I pulled the razor away from his throat just in time.

Try to imagine the scene: I'm standing over a very large man whose face is half-covered with shaving cream, and I'm communicating with a woman he can't see in the mirror in front of him. I really wanted to run away, but I couldn't, so I told him that I was a medium and that Judy was in the spirit world and wanted to give him a message.

It turned out that Judy was the man's wife, and she'd died six months earlier. As I began to describe her, he started to sob. I then asked her if she could give me some evidence that would clinch it for him. She simply said, "Thank you for the lollipops."

I must admit that I was hoping for something more earth-shattering, but her husband broke down completely upon hearing this statement. Two days earlier, he'd gone to visit his wife's grave with their seven-year-old son, who'd asked his father if he could take some lollipops instead of flowers to the grave.

I went on to give the man some more evidence that his wife was still alive in the spirit world, and we talked for almost an hour. He told me that Judy had been so full of love for him and their son that he just knew she was still around them.

By the time I arrived at the Spiritualist church in Edinburgh, I was reminded of why I did mediumship: to prove to people that death isn't the end of human consciousness. That knowledge can heal people whose hearts are breaking.

You Cannot Die for the Life of You

Even though grieving people appear to gain more than anyone else from mediumship, I can't help but think of how many other individuals would benefit from the knowledge that there is life after physical death. I'm sure that this knowledge would shape this world in a much more contented and compassionate way. If we were to lose our fear of death, we'd all live much happier lives as a result.

I know that I have no fear whatsoever of death or what follows—but more important, I have no fear of *living*. This is the real message that I hope my work brings to people.

I've said it many times, but you really cannot die for the life of you. After this physical life has ended, your spiritual life force goes on and on forever, changing and growing as it moves into the spirit world and beyond human comprehension. Mediumship may just offer a little glimpse of what lies ahead, but one thing's for sure: It's a journey we'll all make sooner or later.

⚜ ⚜

Chapter Two

LIFE AFTER DEATH

One of the questions most asked of those in the spirit world has to be: "What's it like over there?" This is natural enough—I mean, aren't you curious? After all, we'll all be going there one day. . . .

When I was beginning to learn about mediumship in my 20s, I assumed that spirit people looked like we do, only a little more glowing. (This, I suppose, was due to how I saw them clairvoyantly.) My instinct told me that the spirit world was a "well-backlit place" filled with shiny, happy people. When I imagined what it looked like, I saw white buildings and a beautiful countryside with colors beyond description. It was easy to accept this, as most of the books I was reading at the time were packed with heavenly realms that fit my own ideas of the hereafter. It wasn't until I managed to find some cassette recordings of a very rare type of phenomenon that my view changed completely.

Voices in the Dark

The mediumship of a man named Leslie Flint was different from anything I'd encountered at that time. When I say "different," I mean that he didn't give messages to his sitters like mental mediums do, or go into a trance and let a highly evolved spirit guide speak through him—and as for ectoplasm, there wasn't even a hint of the controversial misty-white substance around him. It was simply that whenever he sat in a darkened room, voices would be heard in the air around him.

This all began in Leslie's childhood back in the 1920s, when he'd go to watch the silent films at his local movie theater. During the picture, people around him would ask him to be quiet and stop talking, as it was ruining their enjoyment of the film. Leslie never understood this because he could hear the voices, too, only he assumed that they were coming from someone else.

In his late teens, Leslie tried to find out about the strange events that were occurring around him, so he went on to develop his gift in a Spiritualist circle.

It became known as "Independent Direct Voice Mediumship" because the voices were coming directly from the spirit people and were completely independent of the medium. All that was required of Leslie was that he sit in a darkened room.

Now I know that the dark-room bit makes you think *fraud,* but over the years that followed, Leslie Flint was tested by many scientists. Experiments would see our medium tied to a chair, gagged and holding a mouthful of colored water, which he had to empty into a glass at the end of the test to prove that he wasn't a ventriloquist. (If he had been, I'm certain that he could have made a good living on the variety circuit with that kind of act!) Dr. Louis Young invented most of these tests, and along with members of the Society for Psychical Research, carried out additional tests in infrared light with a microphone attached to Leslie's throat. Thus, the voices were recorded.

During the course of many years and many investigations, no one ever accused Leslie Flint of being a trickster or a fake; in fact, his gift became known all over the world. People who had lost a loved one would come from far and wide to see Leslie in the hopes of hearing the voices of their nearest and dearest speak directly to them from beyond the grave. So many people came, as it happened, that Leslie had to hold group sessions to accommodate the demand for sittings.

Each group of people would assemble in the sitting room of Leslie's London flat in anticipation, and spirit people of all descriptions would come and talk to them—and they wouldn't interact solely with their relatives, either. It was as if there was a microphone in the spirit world and those who had crossed over would stand in line waiting for their turn to speak. Voices would come from all corners of the room, and often several entities would converse at once, giving detailed descriptions of their life on Earth and other pieces of personal information. All these sessions were taped, and after listening to many of them myself, I can draw only two conclusions: Either fraud was being carried out by a large group of mimics who could create a wide range of voices and speak in several languages—as well as know a great deal about everyone in each group—or the phenomenon, however unbelievable, was actually happening. I tend to go with the latter.

SPIRITUAL EVOLUTION

Some of Leslie Flint's spirit communicators became regular commentators on their progression in the spirit world, and they'd talk freely to their families about events that had taken place since they last spoke. Common descriptions of the Other Side included being in a great light and feeling a sense of weightlessness and contentment. There was also a sense of being drawn into a brighter light, and if the same spirits had the chance to come and speak at a later session, there was a noticeable sense of development in how they spoke and in their reaction to the material world.

One young man who became a frequent communicator was David Cattanach, who had died at the age of 18. He made many visits to the Leslie Flint sessions over a period of almost ten years, where he spoke to his mother. I know her personally, and she's someone I'd describe as very astute, who wouldn't easily be fooled—especially when it came to her son—and she had no doubts that she was hearing his voice. In his earlier contacts, he spoke mainly to her, giving brief messages of comfort, but also describing his surroundings. At first these were of a fairly material nature, although they were filled with a sense of peace and contentment. But each time he managed to come through, there was a new strength in his voice and brightness in his personality, and there was even a sense of his surroundings changing.

In one of the later sessions, when a member of the group asked David what it was like on the Other Side, he addressed the entire gathering. He started by saying that he couldn't conjure up the words to even begin to describe how beautiful it was there, and that he felt alive in a way that he never had before. He went on to talk about how he'd progressed away from the material world and was now in a state of luminosity. He wasn't aware of having a body anymore—he still had some sort of vehicle, but it wasn't so important.

In his new state, he could expand his knowledge just by encountering another spirit. Everything that they knew was shared with each other, so both could grow in awareness.

David's knowledge certainly seemed to be vast as he described the wonderful levels of consciousness that were open to all to discover. He described death as a great adventure that none of us should fear, and he explained that every level of life was interconnected—and our earthly level was the darkest of them all. He also said that we were limited in our understanding because of our emotions, and that it was important for us to expand our consciousness beyond our limited vision of ourselves.

In the last part of his talk, he spoke to his mother, telling her that no matter how he evolved, they would always be connected. For her, the most marvelous part of these encounters was hearing how her son had grown over the years.

Leslie Flint died in 1991, but most of his work was recorded and can be obtained from the foundation that was set up in his name (**www.LeslieFlint.com**).

Truths and Misconceptions about the Afterlife

Myth #1: White staircases; pearly gates; and Saint Peter with a long, white, flowing beard. . . .

No, these all went out years ago! It's no longer mandatory to wear white flowing gowns, play harpsichords, and hang around on fluffy clouds on the Other Side.

Myth #2: You're likely to receive wings and a halo as a reward for your good deeds or be thrown into hellfire for your bad deeds.

The truth is that this really won't happen.

Myth #3: Heaven will look like Earth with better backlighting, and shiny, happy people will welcome you with hymn singing and tambourine playing.

Contrary to what I once thought, it doesn't, and they won't.

Myth #4: Our Father's kingdom has many mansions set out for individual religious groups.

There are no religious divisions on the Other Side. So, Muslims, Jews, and Christians, you'll all just have to learn to get along over there.

Myth #5: Upon death, you become immediately enlightened.

No, you still have to progress spiritually and take responsibility for your actions in your last human existence.

Myth #6: The spirit world is all there is.

The spirit world is but the first step on your development of consciousness, so don't get too comfortable there.

KNOCKING ON HEAVEN'S DOOR

I can't say that I've actually been to the spirit world, although I have experienced altered states of consciousness, and mental images of it have been imprinted on my mind by spirit communicators. Either way, even though I know that the spirit world exists, I can't give you a true visual image or pinpoint its location. However, descriptions of the hereafter have been given by those who have experienced a near-death experience (NDE) or an out-of-body experience (OBE) (they sound like awards, don't they?).

A typical NDE, as the name would suggest, happens when a person is close to physical death. Many individuals have actually been pronounced dead, only to come back with a tale of their marvelous journey. Now, even though the portrayal may differ from person to person, most have a common thread running through them. First a light appears, which draws the person toward it. This is usually accompanied by a sense of traveling very fast down a tunnel. (Ringing noises may also be heard.)

The journey into the light always seems to end at a point of stillness and contentment. Some say that they see a Christlike figure or angelic beings, while others have given accounts of meeting Buddha or Mohammed; still others see deceased family members. Another common feature is a voice saying that they should go back now, that it's not their time. Most people come back to full consciousness with a feeling of spiritual upliftment and no fear of dying. Often they express great joy at the indescribable sensations they felt while in this altered state of consciousness.

Many such accounts have been investigated over the years, and much has been said about the cause of the experiences being a lack of oxygen in the brain, resulting in hallucinations and a feeling of euphoria. Experiments do contest this, however: Many of those who have experienced NDEs have claimed that they were conscious of conversations going on around them while they were "dead"; others have said their spirit floated upward, and they went on to provide accurate accounts of what they saw in places they couldn't possibly have been to physically. One test involved labels being placed above the lights in the operating room, where they couldn't be seen from the ground, and these were described accurately by several people who claimed to have experienced an NDE.

Recently, I was given general anesthesia before undergoing some very intrusive exploratory tests, and I really hoped that I'd consequently have some sort of paranormal experience. As it happened, I did, but not of the NDE kind. As I began to come to, I became aware of a lot of people standing around me in the recovery room. Some of them were writing, and then I realized that I was speaking. It turned out that I'd been talking during the procedure and had given messages from the spirit world to some of the staff. One of the nurses told me that even though many people mumble a sort of gibberish under anesthesia, I was actually referring to all present by their Christian names and talking about their relatives who had died.

Several of the staff later accompanied me to the recovery room to see if anything more would be said, and then for a laugh, one of the orderlies had asked if I could give them the lottery numbers. Nobody expected an answer, but then I began to spout numbers in quick succession! Quickly, every-one dug into their pockets for a pen and paper!

Even though I had no experience of heaven, maybe one of the hospital staff found material heaven in the following Saturday's lottery drawing. . . .

MY FIRST OUT-OF-BODY EXPERIENCE

Thankfully, I've never had an NDE, but on many occasions I *have* found myself in an out-of-body state. The first time I remember this happening was when I was in my early 20s. I was sitting at my flat in Glasgow when my mind began to drift to memories of my childhood. These were happy thoughts, and I began to feel very relaxed as I drifted down memory lane.

Suddenly, I became aware of a sense of vibration engulfing me. At first I thought that the chair I was in was shaking, but as the vibrations got faster, I knew they had more to do with me. Then I felt as though I were floating up from the chair and moving toward the ceiling. I was aware of how light I'd become and that I was now looking down on some-one, but it took a moment to realize that the person was me!

I have no idea why, but the first thought to enter my mind was about my co-worker Sandra.

No sooner had the thought registered than I was somehow in her bedroom observing her. She was sitting in a basket-weave chair, reading a book and looking very peaceful and calm. Then I noticed the clock on her bedroom wall and shot back into my body with a start.

The sharp return to my body startled me, yet I felt amazing. I assume that the limited thought I had about time was what had brought me back. My body was stone cold, because even though the entire episode felt as though it had taken no more than five seconds, two hours had actually passed.

The following morning I asked Sandra what she'd done the previous evening, and was astounded when she told me that she'd just stayed home and read a book. I had to ask, "Do you have a basket-weave chair in your bedroom?"

"Yes, but how do you know?" she answered with surprise.

It wasn't easy to explain.

HEAVEN KNOWS

It's very difficult for anyone to describe the sensation of being outside their own body, for there are no words to describe the feelings of lightness or stillness experienced in such a state. Similarly, it's difficult for any of us to know what life is like after death. Even with all the spirit communications I've passed between the two worlds, it would appear that everyone who tries to describe their new surroundings gives a different account of what it looks or feels like. Is this because we all perceive things in diverse ways, or because we gravitate to various levels of understanding in the spirit world?

One way of trying to understand what might be going on is to imagine a group of alien visitors coming to our planet, with each one being sent to a different location. One might find oneself situated in the jungles of Africa, another in the middle of New York City, and another on a deserted island in the Caribbean. If each of these visitors tried to describe Earth based on what they'd observed in their own small corner, there wouldn't be any corroboration at all. Each creature would feel that the particular description was accurate, but put together, it couldn't form a complete picture of this planet and all the life that exists on it. What happens in the spirit world may be something along these lines. The best we can do is speculate, as so many people have already done.

For example, the 18th-century scientist Emanuel Swedenborg gave us the theory that upon death, the human spirit is held in a between-life waiting area where it may encounter spirit people who are familiar: family, friends, and associates. His belief was that the spirit would remain in this state for a period, but it would eventually be drawn to a level of like-mindedness, where it would encounter others of a similar essence, according to spiritual merits.

The idea of a between-life state also features in other religious beliefs and practices. For instance, Tibetan Buddhists believe that when we die we must go through what they call the *bardo state,* which is seen as a journey taken by the consciousness at the time of physical death. At that moment, it's said that a clear light will appear, and if we recognize this light, we'll become enlightened. Unfortunately, not many of us do so. However, there are other chances with other five-colored lights that follow. The rule of thumb is to go to the brightest one we see, as the paler, softer lights can lead us in a backward direction. Our consciousness will then move through seven stages of the bardo for a period of 49 days—during which, our consciousness will come face-to-face with many demons, which are projections of our own minds. We must try to accept them rather than run away in fear so that we'll reach the brightest light we can. Whatever state we've reached at the end of 49 days will determine our conscious state at the beginning of our new life.

Both the beliefs of Swedenborg and the practices of the Tibetan Buddhists encourage us to be more aware that we should carry out good actions in this life in order to build up a "spiritual bank balance" to help us in the life to come. Even if both views are wrong, they still encourage us to become better in this life, and that can't be bad.

Having a belief that there's a life after death, no matter what religion or spiritual practice we follow, at least gives us a sense of hope. There are, of course, some people who think that when we die, we're dead, deceased, and defunct. I think that these folks are going to wake up to a great shock on the Other Side, a bit like having a surprise party! Of course, the flip side of this coin was put beautifully by my good friend Professor Archie Roy when he said, "If I find that when I die there's no afterlife, I shall be extremely disappointed."

THE LONG KISS GOOD NIGHT

Robert Parker was a man who had no belief in God, religion, or life after death. After the loss of a son early in his marriage, he became totally opposed to the idea that the human spirit could continue in any way, shape, or form. At the age of 68, having no known illness, he went to bed one night with his wife, Barbara. Before turning to go to sleep, she kissed him on the forehead and said, "Good night." The following morning she was shocked to find that he was dead.

Even though her husband had been totally against the idea of visiting mediums, and on many occasions he'd even ridiculed people who spoke of such things, Barbara couldn't accept the fact that he was gone from her life forever. She decided to look for a reputable medium to see if there was any chance that her husband was wrong about life after death.

I was sitting in a small room in a Spiritualist church in Glasgow waiting for my last appointment of the day, when the door opened and in walked a nicely dressed, good-looking woman in her 60s. I began at once to give her my usual spiel: "Have you had a sitting with a medium before? This is how it works. . . . Please don't give me any information about the person you hope to contact," and so forth. No sooner had I tuned in to the spirit world than I heard a man's voice saying, "I was wrong, I was wrong. Please tell Barbara I was wrong."

Once he got started, there was no stopping this guy! He told me that his name was Bobby, which was how his wife had always referred to him, and that he was with Raymond, who was the son they'd lost early in their marriage. The sitting was packed with information about Bobby's life, with small details that his wife understood and that were relevant to their life together.

Near the end of the sitting, the mood changed somewhat, as Bobby began to relate how he'd found himself in the spirit world. He recalled that he'd gone to bed in his home and had woken up after a beautiful sleep in a room that was filled with light. To his surprise, there was a nurse there holding his long-lost baby son, Raymond. He then talked of meeting his parents and other family members and friends who were dead . . . only they weren't! His wife was able to place all the people he claimed to have met. He gave no great description of his surroundings, but spoke of a state of grace and comfort that he said he couldn't articulate.

The message ended with Bobby reminiscing, "The last thing that you said to me was, 'Good night,' and I remember that you turned and kissed me on the head." He said that this was the first thing he remembered when he woke.

Bobby may have been dead set against the idea of an afterlife, but he's a good example of what mediums have said for years: that you cannot die for the life of you!

GOD'S WAITING ROOM

For most of my adult life, I've tried to understand what it feels like to actually die (I know—it's sad, isn't it?). During that time I've seen, heard, felt, and held conversations with spirit people, at times under the strictest of scientific conditions. I've also experienced leaving my body, being engulfed by white light, and having what I can best describe as *spiritual experiences.* Yet no matter what I've felt or witnessed, I still find it very difficult to comprehend what it's like in the spirit world. No matter how we try to envision it, all we can do is compare it to our earthly lives. Maybe that's why so many of the descriptions of the afterlife still seem to be based on a materialistic world, and involve loving reunions with radiant, departed relatives.

As a medium, I find it hard to believe that when we die we hang around God's waiting room for all our relatives and friends to arrive, with no other purpose than to act as a welcoming committee. I'm sure that there's more to the next life than that. Certainly, though, it would seem that there *is* some kind of reunion with our loved ones. So many nurses and caregivers have witnessed dying people reach out and speak to an unseen person who they claim has come to collect them and take them to the Other Side. Similarly, many of those who have experienced an NDE have mentioned spirit relatives waiting to greet them, as did many of the communicators at the Leslie Flint sessions. There may also be a connection to other individuals who have shared a part of our lives and who have formed a spiritual bond with us.

It's occurred to me that the welcoming committee is there because becoming a spirit in a realm of bright light may be too much for the conscious mind to take in. Is the afterlife so bright that we have to wear shades? We may have to acclimate and limit our view of the true spiritual experience with what our mind can accept at that moment. So the after-life may appear to be a brilliant version of this life until our consciousness can adjust and gravitate to its own level of awareness. Even in this human form, we have the ability to create different views of reality—so often we choose to see what we want to see and not what's real. Does the same apply after death?

I do know that the more we grow in spirit and adapt to our new reality, the less attached we'll become to human ways and conditions, and the clearer our vision will become. From our current standpoint, dying is the most significant event we'll ever have to face, so what can make us more accepting of it? Is it the hope that stems from the knowledge that we live again? Or could it be that we have to reach a point of understanding that we're already spirits, and physical death is no more than a change of environment?

After thinking long and hard about what life will be like when we die, I'm convinced that so much depends on our life now, and on our state of mind at the moment of death. To prepare ourselves for that inevitable journey, we must begin to take responsibility for all that we are in this life, to look at our lives with clarity and assess them with truth. It seems that our delusions about what life holds for us in the hereafter arise from our misconceptions about who we are in the here-and-now. If we can accept that we're already spirit beings living in a spirit realm, we can accept that death isn't so much a journey to a different *world* . . . as it is to a different *state of mind.*

Chapter Three

HEAVEN AND HELL

Some of the most common questions that I'm asked about the afterlife concern heaven and hell. Many people fear that loved ones who have led less-than-perfect lives are held in some "fiery inferno."

For example, on one occasion back in 1996, I was giving a private sitting in London to a middle-aged woman. She was well dressed and looked physically strong and healthy, but her sadness was apparent to me the moment I took her hand. I could instantly hear the voice of a young man in the spirit world telling me that this was his mother.

I sensed the presence of a very tall, slim man in his early 20s, someone who felt awkward, uneasy, and withdrawn. As always, I asked for the name of the communicator, but this time nothing came back to me. So I asked the young man, "How did you die?"

"I don't know," he replied at once.

Whenever I'm communicating with someone who finds it difficult to give information, I ask the spirit world if there's anyone else around who can help them. I'd no sooner sent out this thought than an older lady came through much more strongly. She said her name was Dorothy.

I told my sitter that Dorothy was helping the young man communicate. She looked straight at me and inquired, "Is she?" It turned out that Dorothy was the woman's mother-in-law.

Dorothy passed on a great deal of relevant information about her life and family, including her grandson, whose name was Mike. She explained that he'd been suffering from AIDS and had known that he was going to die very soon. One night he'd simply decided to take some pills from the medicine cabinet and end it all, rather than involve everyone around him in prolonged emotional suffering. His family had already experienced a "social death" from being excluded by other family members, neighbors, and so-called friends.

Then Mike himself began to communicate, telling his mother that he was free of his suffering now and that he wanted to stop her from hurting, too. He knew that she believed he was in some sort of limbo or purgatory because of what he'd done. Such was her torment that she'd consulted a medium, even though it was against her religious beliefs to do so.

In fact, the only hell in this instance was the one Mike's mother had put herself through because of her beliefs and conditioning. Once she was free of this self-imposed prison, a great burden was lifted from her, and she found the freedom to communicate with her son in the spirit world, where he seemed to be happy and at peace.

"Free at Last"

On another occasion in 1996, during a public demonstration I was giving in Spain, a spirit woman communicated with her sister in the audience. She described how she'd never felt loved or appreciated in her marriage and how her life had become hell. In ten years of married life she'd never produced a child, and as a result, she'd felt that her husband had stopped loving her. He was cheating on her and lying about it, and finally she'd simply ended her life by hanging herself. She described her last feelings on Earth as those of a baby lying in a darkened room, alone and screaming for help, with no one around to lift her, care for her, or take away her pain.

Her sister had found her body, and now the spirit woman felt that she had to tell her how sorry she was that her sister had to see her in such a terrible state. She wanted her to try to move on, and not to dwell on the horrible scene she'd encountered. As evidence of her survival, the spirit woman gave names, dates, and addresses relating to her former life, and she also mentioned many events that she'd shared with her sister. She explained that her life on the Other Side was very happy, and she was surrounded by loving people who were helping her progress.

At the end of the demonstration, I made a point of speaking to the sister in private. She told me that she'd been unable to move on with her own life because of the thoght of her sibling suffering in some inferno as the result of the suicide—she'd even offered to trade her own life to try to release her. She told me of her joy at hearing that her sister wasn't in hell or even purgatory after all, but she was instead being helped to move forward. Now the young lady realized that she was prepared to go on with her life and accept happiness again.

I can only conclude from this account that if there truly is such a state of suffering as hell or purgatory, then it exists only in this human world. It's experienced when we're lacking in love, either for ourselves or from those close to us. I can think of no greater emptiness in life than this.

TRUTHS AND MISCONCEPTIONS ABOUT
HEAVEN AND HELL

Myth #1: Hell is a physical place located beneath the ground on this planet.

Surely the earth's surface would have collapsed by now with the number of people being held there, and it would be getting worse by the second . . . so, no to this one.

Myth #2: If you go to hell, you'll roast in everlasting torment.

Again, I don't think so. Fire can only harm the physical body, while the spirit is indestructible and eternal. This is a very human way of looking at suffering in the afterlife.

Myth #3: The devil is a big guy with horns on his head, carrying a large trident and wearing a red outfit.

This wouldn't work, would it? These days, there are characters in children's video games that look more frightening than that!

Myth #4: Heaven is a place where you can indulge in endless sensory pleasures.

No. I'm sorry to disappoint that woman in London who was hoping to meet her many lovers again, but in heaven there's no need for that type of pleasure!

Myth #5: Hell has many levels, such as different units of a prison where the really bad dudes are in the high-security wings, while the lesser offenders are in some sort of open-air division.

No, the real hell isn't subdivided like this. Instead, it's a state experienced by people who are locked in personal torment.

Myth #6: If you sin in this life, you'll go straight to hell, and your soul will be trapped there forever.

Living with the emotional pain we feel in this life when we're aware that we've done wrong has to be punishment enough. If we grow from such an experience, no afterlife judgment is needed.

THE SISTERS GRIM

If we look at both heaven and hell as states of mind, then hell can be perceived as the product of our own way of thinking and our own emotions. Unfortunately, we may come to believe that this is our punishment or just deserts rather than our choice.

An experience that I had when sitting for two sisters in Germany some years ago showed me how some people find it easier to condemn themselves to their own little world of hate than to try to find love. Ida and Irma's sitting began with their father trying to communicate from the Other Side. He told me that he'd been over there for 30 years, but the women just looked at each other, shrugged their shoulders, looked back at me, and said in their heavily accented English, "Why would our father want to speak to us? We hate him!"

I felt rather puzzled, but continued, "He gives me the name of Abe, and says that he'd like to help you."

"Why would he help us now, after so long, when we can't stand him?" they wondered. "What does he really want? Isn't there anybody else we can speak to?"

"Hold on," I said. "Nora Schuster is here. Do you know her?"

At once they called out, "We hate her, too! This is our aunt who brought us up when we were children—why is *she* here?"

I ignored this outburst and proceeded to pass Nora's message on to the sisters, which was that they should look back over their lives and try to understand some of what their family went through for them, then make contact with their brother, Ben, and reunite the family.

At this, both women gave a little shrug, and Ida explained that their Aunt Nora had raised them while their father had devoted all his time to his business. She claimed that Nora had paid more attention to her own children than to Ida and Irma, and said that their older brother had "abandoned" them by going to live in America. What the sisters really wanted to know was whether they'd ever be happy in their lives because they'd been miserable for so many years.

When I heard this last statement, I almost burst out laughing, but I managed to keep my composure. I tried to explain to them that they were creating sadness for themselves and that the hate they felt was only harming them. I asked if they'd like to change their lives and find some form of happiness, and they said that they would. Then I told them to call their brother and see if they could visit him in America.

"But we hate him—," Irma began.

"Stop!" I interrupted. "Please listen to my advice, and think about what I've asked you to do."

The sitting ended with both women looking more miserable than when they'd first entered the room, and I felt that I hadn't done a very good job. But the following morning, I heard voices calling, "Wait, wait!" It was the sisters, both of whom were smiling and running toward me with short little steps. Both grabbed my arm at once and began to tell me their revelation.

It turned out that after much deliberation, they'd called their brother, Ben, in New York, only to find that he was delighted to hear from them. One of his sons was getting married, and his family really wanted to invite their long-lost aunts over for the wedding and to spend time with them. Ben thought that they wouldn't come because they hated him—but to his amazement, they responded that they'd love to attend the wedding and become reacquainted with him and his family. After all, as Ida said, "How could we hate our own family?"

A PAIN IN THE NECK

Of course, taking responsibility for our own behavior isn't always straightforward. It's usually easier to lay the blame on someone else.

Before I demonstrated as a medium, I used to practice spiritual healing in our little Spiritualist church in Glasgow. It was during this time that I first became aware of how some people seemed to be content in their misery. It was excellent training for someone like me, who was trying to bring hope to the hopeless! And I sometimes wondered back then if some of my best healing wasn't done in the salon where I worked. As women who make appointments regularly know, hairstyling is the highest form of counseling—not only can you unload all your troubles, but you come out looking like a million dollars, too!

One of the people I used to see each week at the healing clinic where I assisted was Georgia. She was in her mid-50s and very dowdy. She lived with her husband and son (who was in his early 30s), both of whom were named Tom. Georgia needed healing for the mysterious pain she was suffering at the base of her neck. She'd had every x-ray and examination there was, but no doctor had ever been able to offer a diagnosis.

After each session was over, I'd spend a short time talking to Georgia about her healing and her family. She always seemed down whenever she mentioned both Toms, saying things such as, "They've ruined my life," or "It's because of them that I'm in such pain." I felt so sorry for her, since she always looked so unhappy.

After some months of healing sessions, it was clear to me that my talks with Georgia were increasing in length and frequency, and I felt as if I were becoming part of her life. I knew almost everything about the two men in her life—especially how they didn't include her in anything they did, and how she felt separate from them. She told me that she'd even thought of ending her life, but she feared that would make them happy!

Now, if Georgia had been a client in my salon, I would have advised her to color her hair blonde, change her wardrobe, and demand attention . . . but she wasn't, so I just listened. It became more and more apparent that she wasn't going to make any effort to be happy. In fact, her feelings toward her family were turning into a silent hatred. Along with this, she was suffering more physical pain and even starting to find that her mobility was restricted.

One day I prayed really hard during the healing session that Georgia would be happy and her pains would diminish. Then I suddenly heard myself speaking out loud, telling her that she'd have to learn to make her own happiness and include herself in the lives of her husband and son. Once I'd begun, there was no stopping me, and by the end of the session, Georgia was in tears. She said that she knew she was causing her own misery and creating hell in her home. Her husband didn't know what to do with her, and her son feared her frequent rages. She'd been pushing both men away from her, and she knew it. No matter how many times she tried to blame them, inside she could feel that it was all her fault.

As soon as Georgia admitted that she was responsible for her problems, she felt a weight lift from her shoulders. Over the weeks that followed, she became stronger and more positive. For our last session, she even turned up with tastefully styled hair and a smart skirt and blouse, and she looked so happy and alive. She thanked me for all the healing and told me that she and Tom, Sr., were going off on vacation. Then she remarked, "I feel as though I'm in heaven!"

To witness such a change of heart is wonderful. So many people never seem to progress emotionally or mentally in life, yet no state of mind is permanent unless we choose to make it so. By examining our thinking and exercising some control over our emotions, we can all gain enough awareness to break free from our negative patterns. Each and every one of us encounters difficult experiences in our lives, but we can learn to grow from them.

"WALKING A STEP BEHIND"

The shock of bereavement is a difficult experience that can affect our state of mind a great deal, even take us into a different state of consciousness that may be our own personal form of hell. One woman who had recently lost her young son in a terrible automobile accident described this to me very vividly.

"I feel as if I'm walking a step behind my body," she began, "and my thinking is out of sync with the places and people I encounter. Even when people speak to me, I become aware of what they're thinking more than what they're saying, as if I've become stuck in a world of thought and am unable to become a part of real life again."

This reminded me of how we mediums feel when we experience an altered state of consciousness in order to make a stronger link with the spirit world. While in this state, we'll experience a feeling of separateness from our bodies and a sense of being out of reality. Our sensitivity heightens in such a way that we become more in tune with a more subtle atmosphere.

The grieving woman even talked about a kind of numbness, like being in limbo, which she felt was safe because while in this state she neither had to look back nor forward. Her limbo had become a haven away from "normality." Even in this mental void, however, something deep down was nagging away at her to get back into life.

Our sitting had a big effect on her: "It was like electricity hitting me, bringing me back to life," she told me. This was the spirit of her son affecting her consciousness and jump-starting it back into human reality. (Again, this type of electrical surge is felt by trance mediums when we flit from one state of consciousness to another.) The upshot of the experience was that the woman no longer felt disconnected and alone in her grief, but was prepared to reenter normal reality. Tough as that would be, she was no longer in a state of limbo.

JUDGMENT DAY

So many views of the afterlife are based on the idea of a judgment, after which the "good" people go to heaven and the "bad" people go to hell. But who is all good or all bad in life? How good do we have to be to get through the pearly gates, and what's bad enough for the eternal toasting? If decent young people get sent off to war and are asked to kill other decent young people in the name of democracy, is this worthy of an eternal stay in the flames of hell, or are they granted a get-out-of-jail-free card on some moral technicality? And who decides?

While attending a book signing by a well-known psychic in Glasgow, I asked him if he'd ever seen or sensed someone from the spirit world. He told the packed bookstore that he hoped he never would because when he was a young man doing national service for his country, he'd killed someone on the opposing side. He explained that it was a case of "kill or be killed," but that memory had haunted him ever since, and he wondered if he'd have to face the young soldier when he died. Isn't it hell to try to live with such a heavy burden? And is that enough, or should this man be punished further after death? I believe that the remorse he feels in this life, and what he's learned from the situation, will balance out his karmic debt.

One of the Spiritualist religion's principles, which I know is echoed in other spiritual practices, is that we should take personal responsibility for our own actions. This is how we measure our growth in this life. When I'm asked where "bad" people will go in the next life, I try to explain that people aren't really bad when they come into this world, but they may carry out bad actions—and that's simply human nature at work. We all make mistakes. To become aware of them and admit them is a way of lightening our load and moving forward. To repeat the same things time after time is foolish and can be seen as not learning our lessons.

As I understand it, in this lifetime we'll experience both heaven and hell, love and hate. We'll all feel the full spectrum of emotions and move through our own heavens and hells, but learning to accept and grow from them is the natural journey our consciousness wants to make.

We're all capable of creating either heaven or hell: Both belong in this human existence, and both are simply experiences that we can learn from.

※ ※

Chapter Four

GHOSTS AND SPIRITS

*P*eople have always been fascinated by things that go bump in the night. Children especially seem to love the suspense of a good ghost story—even my sons used to ask me to tell them such tales when they were younger, but now I think they'd be more reluctant to do so, in case they got the real thing!

The idea of anyone, or anything, for that matter, returning from beyond the grave is usually seen as creepy and horrible. It's as if we've been programmed to think that anything coming back from the dead is evil and wants to steal our souls. We frighten ourselves even more with our own imaginings—after all, any child in a darkened bedroom can turn a white shirt on a doorknob into a ghost or ghoul.

If only people understood the real phenomena, they could tell their children that where ghosts and spirits are concerned, there really is nothing to be afraid of . . . the fear we feel comes from ourselves.

This was the case with my first official haunting.

My First Haunted House

Not long after I'd begun to work as a medium, my teacher, Mrs. Primrose, took me along to a house where a family was being disturbed by what they said was the ghost of an old man. His appearances were becoming increasingly frequent and were being experienced by more and more people.

I'd never been to an official haunting before, and I remember asking Mrs. P. what we could expect during our encounter with the elderly phantom. She explained that we'd ask each person to give an account of what they'd experienced; try to put together a picture of the ghost to find out if there was any particular reason that he was appearing to this family; then, if need be, we'd tune in to the spirit world and find out if there was any spiritual activity that needed to be addressed. Then we'd determine if what was happening was "just a ghost" or a figment of the imagination of the people concerned.

We arrived at the surprisingly modern home. (I suppose I thought it would be a creaky old house standing next to its own cemetery.) Mr. and Mrs. Thompson and their teenage son and daughter were standing in the small front hall, along with their neighbor, who had also seen the alleged ghost. Mrs. P. questioned each person in turn, while I listened. All the accounts were practically identical: Around 9 P.M., an elderly man was seen wearing a white shirt and dark pants with old-fashioned suspenders hanging at the side. Everyone agreed that he'd appear for a few seconds and then vanish into thin air.

Mrs. P. had a strong sense that there wasn't a spirit trying to communicate or get noticed for any reason here, but she said that she'd tune in to see if she could sense any psychic history in the area of the sightings. I watched as she closed her eyes for a moment and then spoke about a farm and "James Patterson," who had died alone and very sad. She also gave other details about Mr. Patterson's life, which I noted for further investigation.

Next, Mrs. Primrose spoke to the group and told them that they had nothing to worry about because what they were seeing was "only a ghost." (I remember thinking, *Only a ghost!*) Mrs. P. explained that this was just a memory of someone's life trapped in time, and even though it might be seen again, it couldn't interact with this world—it was only a visual phenomenon, not a spirit, angry or otherwise.

The Thompson family and their neighbor seemed to be quite relieved by this explanation and thanked us both for coming. Mr. Thompson said that he'd try to find out some of the history of the place to see if he could trace Mr. Patterson and the farm.

It must have been about two weeks later when Mr. and Mrs. Thompson came along to our Spiritualist church to see Mrs. Primrose. They explained that they'd looked into the history of the land on which their home was built, and they'd been astonished to find the following: According to old building plans, the very spot where their ghost appeared was previously part of an old farmhouse. It was even more surprising for them to learn that the last owners of the farm, some 20 years earlier, had been a Mr. and Mrs. J. Patterson. In addition, they told us that since Mrs. P. and I had visited their home, there had been no more sightings of the ghost.

Ghostly activity such as this can be triggered by someone giving off strong emotional vibes, and of course when others learn about it they become frightened, which helps set it off again. Often when the fear factor is removed, the phenomenon ceases, as it did in this case.

Such phantomlike visions seem to be programmed to play out past actions that have taken place at that spot. They're a memory trapped in time that can be replayed, given the right conditions—in much the same way that a videotape can be repeatedly viewed whenever the PLAY button is pressed.

You have to wonder what could cause such a thing to happen, but most people who have seen ghosts have reported that they appear to be in a highly emotional state. If this is so, then all that's being witnessed is the "stain" or memory of an emotional episode in a person's life, which has left its impression on a time and place.

This, I feel, accounts for two things that often feature in sightings of ghosts: (1) The appearance of phantoms screaming as if in pain, appearing to be very somber and depressed, or even looking as if they don't have heads; or (2) the strong emotions such as fear, depression, or rage that are often felt by the people witnessing these apparitions. Is this because it isn't only the audiovisual impressions that have been trapped, but the emotional anguish as well? If a person can remember his or her own mental state at the time of their encounter with a ghost, it can make it easier to understand the emotional telepathy that flipped the "ghost switch" and caused the videotape to be played again.

Not all reports of apparitions turn out to be of the ghostly kind, however. On some occasions, visions speak to people or give messages. These aren't ghosts, but spirits who have returned for some reason.

THE BLUE RING

One Sunday in December 1994, I took my sons for a drive to Callander, a small town about an hour from Glasgow. While I was there, I found myself looking in an old junk shop. My son Steven was drawn to a ring made of lapis lazuli in one of the glass cases, and he asked me if I'd buy it for him. Wondering why he wanted such a thing, I asked the sales clerk if I could take it from the case for him to try on. Then Steven said that it wasn't for him, but I should have it. I must admit that when I picked up the ring, I really did like it, but I decided that if it fit, I'd buy it. I tried it on, but it didn't fit any of my fingers, much to Steven's disappointment. The clerk told me that it was the only one she had and that she couldn't even remember where it had come from. When we left the store, I told my son that I'd look for another ring like it, and he simply said, "You'll get one soon, Dad."

The following evening, my old teacher, Mrs. Primrose, was in her little flat preparing Christmas gifts for her family and friends. She left them all neatly piled on her sideboard, each labeled with a tag bearing the name of the recipient—except for my present, which was just a tag with my name and number left atop her telephone. Then she sat in her chair and gracefully passed into the spirit world. The following morning she was found by her help, who called to tell me that she'd found my name and number where Mrs. P. had left it. I was shocked when I was told of the news, but when I learned that Mrs. P. had a broad smile across her face, I knew that she'd be fine on the Other Side.

That evening Mrs. P.'s daughter, May, told me that her mother had left a gift for everyone she knew but me. She'd found this rather strange because she was certain that her mother would have wanted me to have something, but I assured her that she'd given me enough in life to remember her by.

The following day, I had a phone call from my psychic-artist friend Dronma. She asked me if Mrs. Primrose had died, for she'd appeared in Dronma's bedroom in spirit form in the early hours of the morning, smiling broadly. Mrs. P. had spoken to her calmly, asking Dronma if she could go to Callander and buy a blue ring for me from the old junk shop there.

Amazed by what Dronma had said, I explained about the ring I'd seen in Callander the day before Mrs. P.'s passing. However, I told her that it didn't fit me, so she needn't bother going to get it. I was too late, for Dronma had already driven over early that morning—Mrs. Primrose had insisted that the ring was to be my Christmas gift from her.

As bizarre as all this seems, I can assure you that every bit of it is true, yet the strangest part of this story happened when I actually received the ring.

Since it didn't fit my fingers, and there's no way I could have a ring made of stone adjusted, I thought I'd wear it around my neck on a chain. However, when the ring was handed to me, my first reaction was to try it on my middle finger, and even though it had previously been too big, it now fit as if made specially for that finger.

When Mrs. P. died, I thought I'd somehow hear from her again, but I didn't think it would be so soon . . . and how clever she was to appear to Dronma, who lives in a village next to Callander!

Spirit people tend to like to tie up their unfinished business and, if they can, help people that they've left behind. They usually don't appear just for the sake of it; in fact, very often they'll appear to someone other than close family or friends because otherwise their loved ones might believe that they'd just created the visit out of their own emotional need.

RETURN TO THE SHOPKEEPER

Tricia Robertson is the vice president of the Scottish Society for Psychical Research (SSPR), the secretary of PRISM (Psychical Research Involving Selected Mediums), and the co-author of two scientific papers on psychical research. She's investigated many different cases of psychic phenomena, many of which are listed in her forthcoming book, *The Uninvited.*

The account that follows is from Tricia's book and deals with what I call "spirit return":

A shopkeeper, Muhammad Khan, known to me for many years, was recently redecorating a room in his home and was painting quite happily at the highest point of a bedroom ceiling when suddenly there he was, four feet away from his face: a customer who used to come into his shop. He was at the same height from the floor, just under ceiling level, and about four feet away horizontally. Khan noted that he was only visible from the waist upwards, was wearing an olive green shirt and a tweed jacket and that his face was totally lifelike.

This vision then pointed at him and said, in a very animated manner, "Tell them not to do it—everything will be all right." In a state of shock, Khan simply stared at him. He repeated his message adamantly and then disappeared just as quickly as he had appeared.

Shaking with shock and disbelief, Khan came down the ladder very slowly, as he was in grave danger of falling off it, and even after several cups of tea he was unable to do any more work that evening. He thought back and realized that this man had died over six years ago.

The next day he attended to his shop as usual and was happy to forget the happenings of the previous evening, however the following day the widow of the "apparition" came into the shop and this posed a serious problem—should he tell her about his experience or not? He eventually plucked up the courage. Her reaction was to throw her arms around him and thank him, saying that she had already been given similar information by someone else and this confirmed it. Khan was bewildered, as he did not have a clue as to what it was all about.

About two weeks later this lady offered an explanation. It transpired that her son had been wrongly accused of a crime and the family had thought of taking him to Ireland to hide, which would obviously have meant that he could not appear at court. Had they done so, the young man would have been in trouble for the rest of his life, but when he did finally appear in court, contrary to all their expectations, the case was dismissed.

Khan had never experienced anything like this before and has not done so since and he is known to me as a trustworthy person. In case the sceptic [sic] thinks that he rushed to tell me of this tale, he did not. It was only during a chance conversation with him that these details emerged and he only told it to me in the knowledge that I would not think that he had gone completely crazy.

I never did ask if the redecoration of the room was ever completed!

In this case, the spirit was returning to give advice that would help his family in a time of great need. Why he chose this particular man and in this particular situation, who can say? Maybe his wife would have put it down to wishful thinking if she'd experienced it herself. What I *am* certain of is that this was no ghost—instead, it was a spirit that was still conscious and concerned about the welfare of his family.

I've often found that spirits are drawn to us in when we're going through rough times. It's not that they're watching us every minute of the day, but it's when we need them most that they seem to be closest to us. Now, such apparitions may be startling, but they shouldn't be seen as evil or malevolent. Cases of "spirit return" normally bring comfort and don't leave any sense of fear. If the information the spirits give is helpful, then the experience should be looked on as a completely positive one.

THE NIGHT SHIFT

There are many reasons why spirits return—but more often than not, all they wish to do is comfort us or try to guide a loved one. The fear we feel isn't because the spirit has come to frighten us; it has more to do with the unexpected nature of the experience. Even as a tried-and-tested medium who's used to encountering spirit people, I still get a jolt if I wake in the early hours and find someone standing beside my bed just looking into my face. I'd often jump with fright when I'd awaken to find my son Steven, who was about three years old at the time, standing beside my bed staring at me. Anyone whose child has done this will know what I mean! That fear is similar to suddenly seeing a spirit, but once you become accustomed to what's happening, the terror immediately goes away.

A friend of mine once asked if I'd come to her home to validate what she'd been experiencing.

It turns out that she kept feeling as if someone was standing in her bedroom, which was disturbing her sleep and leaving her exhausted in the morning.

When I went into her room, I immediately felt the presence of a spirit lady next to the dressing table that stood opposite the bed. Within seconds she was communicating with me, so I knew at once that this wasn't a ghost. She told me that she was my friend's aunt, and she'd only come to be close to her because my friend had just ended a relationship with her boyfriend and would cry herself to sleep at night. She'd get close to her niece, who would then wake up and become frightened. The fear of being haunted would fill my friend's mind and keep her awake until daylight.

When she found out that it was her loving aunt who was coming to watch over her, my friend lost all her fear. She confessed that she'd thought it was the ghost of a murderer who was trying to kill her! She also told me that her aunt had worked as a nurse and preferred to work the night shift, so it was a habit of hers, I suppose, to look in on people after dark.

TRUTHS AND MISCONCEPTIONS ABOUT GHOSTS AND SPIRITS

Myth #1: Ghosts look like people covered with a white sheet, with holes cut out for the eyes and mouth.

I think that this image belongs to a different kind of organization! And a ghost will never say "Boo!" to frighten you.

Myth #2: The function of ghosts is to come to give messages from the hereafter.

No, they're no more than memories trapped in time and place.

Myth #3: Ghosts walk through walls.

If it seems as though they do, it's only because that wall didn't exist in their time frame.

Myth #4: Ghosts set out to frighten people.

People usually become afraid because of the sudden ghostly activity, that's all.

Myth #5: An exorcism or high religious ritual will rid you of a ghost.

No, the only way to stop a spirit is to find out what emotion in you set it off, and then to change the way you feel.

Myth #6: Spirits who have returned from beyond the grave look like rotting corpses or zombies.

Sometimes spirits are transparent, but they usually just look like normal people—and they certainly wouldn't be caught dead at a haunted house!

THE HOODED MONKS

A classic ghost sighting that recently came to my attention has been taking place in a residential care facility for adults with learning difficulties in the southwest of Scotland. The night-duty staff claimed to hear footsteps when there was no one around and voices speaking in whispers in one of the corridors, and they reported seeing a shadowy figure on a wall, which always just appears, passes by, and then disappears.

The most common complaint has been that of a hooded monk. In fact, it turns out that there have been several different descriptions of this monk: Some say that his hood is one color, while others say it's another; in fact, the hood may differ, as does the size of the figure himself.

One of the best witnesses interviewed by the psychic researchers investigating the case was one of the day attendants. She claimed to have entered her office to find a tall, thin, bearded man wearing a brown monk's robe standing right in front of her. He went about his business as if she wasn't there, or perhaps he was unaware of her. She was startled, but picked up a feeling of sadness from him.

This case is still being investigated, but what's gone on in this very ordinary modern building is typical of ghostly activities. It's become more interesting of late because the investigators have recently discovered that the home was built on the site of an orchard that once belonged to an adjoining church, which for a time was used by different orders of monks who visited this part of Scotland from many parts of the world. This may explain the varied descriptions of the robes and hoods.

Again, as is common with this type of haunting, the characters and events belong in another time, and even though they might encroach on this dimension, there's no interaction between the two.

LAST ORDERS

Not long ago, I was invited to an old pub just outside Glasgow, where the staff had been complaining about ghosts and other spooky happenings. It just so happened that I was taking part in some filming for a television program at the time, and everyone involved agreed to allow the "ghost-busting" to be filmed.

The pub was a typical one, with a small bar area

leading through to a larger lounge area. Nothing looked out of the ordinary until the film crew, the psychic investigators, and I were led up an old staircase into an abandoned room above the pub. As is customary when I work with psychic researchers, I wasn't given any information about the nature of the haunting; however, statements had been taken from all the people concerned who had experienced the paranormal events.

The room was dark and dusty and hadn't been in use for many years by the look of it, but as a medium, I had to put the physical surroundings out of my mind and tune in to the finer energies present. I was immediately drawn to the far wall of the room, where there was a hole where a fireplace once was, but my intuition told me that there were no spirits of the past lingering there. I stopped and mentally asked if there were any spirits wishing to communicate—when I felt nothing, I tuned in psychically to read some of the emotional history of the place. All the while, the cameras were rolling and the researchers were listening to see if I could corroborate any of the stories given by the pub's staff.

In my mind's eye, I could see an elderly man standing against the fireplace and then sitting down on a bench beside it as he spoke to someone very young. I knew that the original fireplace was still in the pub somewhere (it had been taken from this room and moved to another). I heard loud footsteps walking across the floor, but I still felt no spirit presence. Nevertheless, I did pick up the names "Jimmy Reid" and "Lizzie Mac," who the manager told me were people in his family. Uncle Jimmy used to own the building in which we stood, and he'd been dead for many years; however, Lizzie, his wife, was still alive.

Now this is where it all got strange. It became apparent to me why I was there, so I told the manager that I sensed nothing untoward or threatening about the place, but that there was someone on the Other Side who wished to make contact with Lizzie.

As far as the haunting of the building went, several of the pub's staff had heard footsteps in the room above them when they were alone, and one young boy said that an elderly man had come and sat beside the fireplace in the downstairs bar—he could even hear the old man speaking, as though he were rambling in a past conversation. It turned out that that very fireplace had come from the room upstairs where I'd sensed it. All these events relating to the old building were stored in the atmosphere of the old place, but I'd sensed separately that the previous owner, Lizzie, had someone in the spirit world who wished to communicate with her and had taken the opportunity to make this known to me.

The film crew and all the other people involved sat chatting in the bar after we'd finished filming, and I was approached by the manager, who wondered if it would be possible for me to see his Aunt Lizzie at some point in the future.

Two weeks later, I gave a private sitting to Lizzie Mac. Her husband in the spirit world had spent most of his life running the "haunted pub" with his wife, and had passed away just two years earlier. He told me that he knew how much she missed him, so he'd had to get back to convince her that he was still around.

As Lizzie said herself: "I might have known he'd still be hanging around that bar!"

Things That Go Bump in the Night

Things that go bump in the night always send a shiver down our spines, but it's often just our lack of understanding that makes us afraid, rather than the paranormal events themselves. On all the occasions that I've helped investigate cases of hauntings, ghosts, and so-called earthbound spirits, I've never come across anything that left me scared. I admit that there have been moments when I've been startled by a sudden noise or vision—for example, when an object has moved or floated in front of me, defying the laws of physics. But because I understand what's going on, I still manage to accept the situation and try to tune in to the unseen energies to discover what's behind it all.

More often than not, I feel quite relieved when I'm asked to go someplace where people are frightened of a particular phenomenon, and I can help them understand or remove it—which is usually the case with more powerful disturbances from unseen forces. There are times I've felt like a "psychic exterminator" when I'm asked to get rid of pesky disturbances. But my motto has become "The more I experience, the less I fear."

Like the child who imagines all sorts of monsters in a darkened room at night, we must learn that to get rid of the monsters, we only have to put on the light: in this case, the light of understanding.

Chapter Five

POLTERGEISTS AND HAUNTINGS

Poltergeist activities and hauntings are very different from apparitions of ghosts and spirits. Yes, it's amazing to witness furniture or ornaments and other objects moving independently around a room as if being pushed or lifted by an invisible force—yet there's always an explanation for such activity if you look for it.

MAXWELL PARK

I was just 12 years old when I first heard the word *poltergeist*. At that time all the newspapers in Scotland were reporting on the paranormal activity in a house near where I was brought up. One of the boys involved in this case went to my school, and kids being what they are, most of us poked fun at him about the ghostly carryings-on. I later became acquainted with one of the psychic researchers who had investigated the case, Professor Archie Roy of Glasgow University, whose account of the case can be found in his book *A Sense of Something Strange*. (Today Professor Roy is not only a good friend of mine, but he's also one of the leading authorities on psychic research.)

The three families involved, whose names have been changed for obvious reasons, were the Uppinghams and the Downies, who lived in the Maxwell Park area of Glasgow; and the Schwarz family, who lived about a quarter of a mile away. Mrs. Schwarz was the sister of Mrs. Uppingham.

Mr. and Mrs. Uppingham were between 40 and 45 years of age, and they lived on the second floor of the house in Maxwell Park with their sons— 14-year-old Ian, who was in the year ahead of me at school, and David, 11—as well as Mrs. Uppingham's mother, who was 70. In the flat beneath them lived Mr. and Mrs. Downie, who were both in their late 60s, and their son, Frank, who was about 30.

The first phase of poltergeist phenomena began in November 1974. The Uppinghams started hearing banging sounds echoing around their home, which they felt sure were coming from the flat downstairs. Finally, Mr. Uppingham could stand it no longer, so he called the police. When the officers arrived, they asked the Downie family about the disturbance, but Mr. Downie claimed that the noise was coming from the flat above and not from his. The police gave him a warning and left.

Within a short period of time, Mr. Uppingham called the police to report that the noise had gotten louder. This time the Downie family was taken to the station for questioning, but the noises continued. For the first time, Mr. Uppingham realized that something more was involved in this disturbance.

In the days that followed, all sorts of people became involved—carpenters, plumbers, electricians, and other building specialists, as well as people from the town council—as they all tried to determine a logical explanation for the problem. Nothing was found, and the disturbances continued . . . only now a new phase had started: Objects were being lifted by an unseen force and thrown around the rooms in the upstairs flat. It was so disturbing that the Uppingham family fled to their relatives, the Schwarz family. However, as Professor Roy says, "Of course, in true poltergeist fashion, whatever it was moved with them and set up home in the Schwarz house."

It was at this point that the Faculty of Divinity from the University of Glasgow was called in to conduct a service at Maxwell Park, assisted by Rev.

Max Magee. The service was successful in ending the phenomena there; however, at the Schwarz house, the strange occurrences were being seen by more and more people. At first, some of the witnesses believed the activity to be some form of trickery, but they eventually became convinced that it was, in fact, paranormal. A local priest was asked to perform an exorcism there, and after that, all appeared to be calm. Relieved, the Uppinghams moved back to Maxwell Park.

Nevertheless, the disturbances started all over again: Items were thrown, the banging became even louder, and tables started to levitate. (Rev. Magee and Professor Roy witnessed many of these phenomena and recorded them on audiotape.) Then a third phase began, which concerned everyone, since the two boys, Ian and David Uppingham, started experiencing spontaneous contortions of their bodies.

Spiritualist mediums were now invited to hold séances to rid the building of evil spirits, for it was Mrs. Uppingham's belief that the house was built over an abandoned mineshaft and that the spirits of miners who had been killed during an accident many years before were trapped or angry. All sorts of other theories were also produced, most of which involved bad or trapped spirits. There's no doubt that there were indeed paranormal happenings in the house at Maxwell Park, but to blame all of them on the spirits of miners who may or may not have died somewhere in the vicinity would be foolish. It seemed in this case, as in so many others, that the people involved never looked to themselves for the answers. After all, it always seems easier to involve disturbed souls who are held between two worlds.

Ultimately, the poltergeist activity stopped almost as suddenly as it had begun, when Ian Uppingham was sent away to live for a while with relatives in the north of Scotland—by this point, both Professor Roy and Rev. Magee had formed the firm opinion that Ian was the main focus of the phenomena. Although Professor Roy couldn't be sure that this course of action had cured the situation, everything did seem to become much quieter after the boy left. And so, even in this very distressing case, the investigators were of the opinion that the paranormal activity, however extreme, was not of another world, but caused by someone in *this* one.

When it comes to poltergeist activity, I consider it almost the opposite of the ghost phenomenon, which is an emotional episode trapped in time and place: A poltergeist is an explosion of emotion from deep within the mind of a person who's trying to imprison his or her own emotions. Such deep feelings tend to escape and build into a sort of telekinetic force that manifests around the troubled person.

LITTLE VOICE

So what do you do if you're faced with such a situation? Some people report these types of experiences to the Society for Psychical Research (SPR) in Great Britain and in many other countries around the world. But not that many people know about the SPR, so let's face it, when it comes to ghostbusting, "who you gonna call?"

A large percentage of people who find themselves in this type of situation speak to a minister or priest, or even a medium or psychic. For example, our little Spiritualist church in Glasgow often had people asking for help with hauntings and other strange occurrences in their homes or places of work.

Mrs. Primrose, the leader of our church, would attend any so-called disturbances of a paranormal nature when she could, but her first rule was that in such cases you must never work alone because you need verification if there really are paranormal phenomena taking place, and because, as a medium, you'd have to tune in and would need someone with you who would remain alert at all times. For these and other reasons, there were three of us, including Mrs. P., at 33 The Crescent, back in 1993, to investigate a young couple's claims that their new home was haunted.

This average couple in their 20s lived in what looked like a very ordinary bungalow in the Glasgow area, except that they claimed objects would move of their own accord, banging noises could be heard at all times of the day and night, and toys that belonged to their two-year-old daughter would move around frequently when no one was near them.

Mrs. Primrose interviewed the couple separately, and it was clear that both had witnessed the same phenomena, sometimes together and other times individually. Both were clearly disturbed by what they'd seen and heard—and what was worse was the fact that the wife was experiencing a sense of being held around her neck as she lay in bed.

Mrs. P. was just about to tune in and see whether she could feel any spirit people when an ornament sitting on a low table began to turn and move toward the edge, where it appeared to float for a moment before it landed softly on the carpet. Seconds afterward, a small toy piano started to play by itself. Every one of us could see the small keys moving and hear the music, but there was no particular tune. The scene was bizarre, to say the least.

Then thumping sounds could be heard coming from around the bottom half of the living-room door, and with this I heard a child's voice saying, "Mama." I looked around at the others in the room to see their reactions; when no one mentioned it, I whispered to Mrs. Primrose what I was hearing. Then everything stopped, and at that moment I became aware of a small boy in the spirit world.

Mrs. P. and I took the woman into the bedroom, and my teacher asked me to tell the young lady what I was sensing. As I did, I sensed the child strongly again—so I described him as being around four years old, having beautiful blond curls and big blue eyes, and looking like a fit little boy of that age.

I then got the sense that he'd died three or so years ago, and the person he was addressing as "Mama" was the young lady. Her face was very red and she had tears running down the sides of her cheeks, but she said nothing. It was when I said that he wanted the toy elephant that she broke down sobbing. She explained to us that three years previously her little boy, who was just less than a year old, had died due to a heart defect. This was eight months before she'd met her husband. For some reason, she'd never mentioned to him that she'd been in an earlier relationship and had lost her little boy. In fact, the only thing she'd kept to remind her of her son was a little toy elephant that lay on her pillow, which she held each night before going to sleep.

I'm sure that the woman had her own reasons for not telling her new husband about her baby, but it was clear to me that, although she may have thought she'd put her little boy out of her mind, he was obviously not out of her heart . . . or her life, for that matter. All the activity that was occurring in her home was consistent with the behavior of a small child: objects being lifted from low tables, banging sounds coming from the floor or the bottom halves of the walls and doors, something wrapping itself around the woman's neck as she lay in bed, and the toys often being moved (or should I say "played with"?). It's bad enough when you can see a kid moving things all over the place, but try to imagine how it would appear if an invisible child was causing the same disruption. I can see why the couple felt disturbed by the activities, but when they knew it was a tyke in the spirit world who was responsible, their view changed at once.

A week later, Mrs. P. received a letter from the young woman explaining that she'd told her husband everything about the baby and her previous relationship. Apparently, she'd hoped that she could block it all out of her mind, but her love for her lost child and the grief she'd never allowed herself to feel had seemingly caused some of the psychic activity. When I last heard from the couple (which was quite recently), there had been no more disturbances in their home—except for the arrival of a new baby boy.

Attention, Please!

In cases of poltergeist activity, there's usually somebody who's crying out for attention, either in the unseen world or this one. One of the most famous in Britain was known as the "Enfield Poltergeist." It started back in 1977 when Mrs. Peggy Harper, a divorcée in her mid-40s, was called by her 11-year-old daughter, Janet, and her 10-year-old son, Pete, to their bedroom. They claimed that banging noises were keeping them awake.

Mrs. Harper looked around the room for signs of anything that could cause the ruckus, but saw nothing untoward. She left the room, closing the door behind her—but no sooner had she done so than a loud noise echoed from the bedroom. When she reentered, to her shock, a large set of drawers moved of its own accord some two feet from the wall, and banging could be heard coming from the back wall, which adjoined the neighbor's home.

Mrs. Harper removed both children from the bedroom and sent for her next-door neighbors, who also witnessed the moving of furniture and the clamor. Then the police were called: The officers also heard the unexplained sounds, and one of them even saw a chair inexplicably move across the floor, along with small plastic bricks and marbles being thrown around the room by some sort of invisible hand.

So intense were the phenomena that a minister was called for, then a local medium was brought in, and finally the Society for Psychical Research was consulted. Maurice Grosse, a researcher for the SPR, attended this case for two years and witnessed all sorts of paranormal activity, from electrical faults and the unexplained mechanical failure of filming equipment to objects being hurled around rooms and bedclothes being mysteriously pulled off the children's beds. He even recorded voices speaking through the little girl, Janet. There were also reports of Janet levitating out of her bed, which was also witnessed by one of the neighbors.

The case was widely reported and became the subject of TV programs. At one point young Janet was taken to the hospital for tests; while she was gone (a period of about six weeks), the phenomena stopped.

Some two years later, interest in the case began to fade—when this happened, the psychic activity ceased. The investigators thought that the activity was somehow caused by Janet, as she seemed to be at the center of it all, and it didn't happen when she wasn't around. Janet was one of four children being brought up by a single mother, so a lot of attention was probably not heaped on her—again, a major factor in a case of poltergeist activity.

Poltergeist phenomena are usually associated with children or teenagers, often those starting puberty or menstruation, as Janet was in this case. It may be that the emotional changes and the buildup of intense feelings somehow cause telekinetic activity in which objects move around and strange banging sounds are heard. I feel that all this stems from the child's need for attention or affection. Often the children involved are said to be withdrawn or shy—well, outwardly they may be quiet and calm, but inside there is emotional turbulence, which explodes as poltergeist activity when they crave attention.

The problem with cases of psychic phenomena involving kids is that when a child is singled out as being the cause, even if the events were of a paranormal nature to begin with, there's always the chance that he or she may invent more episodes to keep people interested.

TRUTHS AND MISCONCEPTIONS ABOUT POLTERGEISTS AND HAUNTINGS

Myth #1: If an object has moved a little from its original place in your home or you can't always find the items you're looking for, a poltergeist must be to blame.

Don't call the ghostbusters; it's probably that you're becoming a wee bit forgetful. Real cases of poltergeist phenomena are very rare—and believe me, you'd know if you had the real thing.

Myth #2: Loud, banging sounds in your home mean that it's haunted.

More often than not, your central heating is on the blink or there's some other rational explanation.

Myth #3: Children who behave badly and use foul language must be possessed.

They probably just watch too much late-night television or play too many violent video games. Oh, and never feed them pea soup before bed!

Myth #4: Hollywood movies portray hauntings in an accurate manner.

No, genuine cases of poltergeist-type hauntings don't feature A-list actors, and they don't tend to take place in houses built over ancient Indian burial grounds.

Myth #5: A poltergeist is an evil spirit.

It's far more likely to be telekinetic activity caused by a child suffering some deep emotional trauma.

Myth #6: Priests, ministers, psychic researchers, or mediums should be called in immediately.

Most cases of poltergeist activity burn themselves out in a very short period of time. The less attention given to a poltergeist, the better—starving it of attention is the surest way to make it stop.

A Funny Thing Happened
on the Way to the Haunting

Not all cases of poltergeist activity investigated by mediums and psychic researchers are as spectacular as that of the Enfield Poltergeist. Most of the cases I've gone to could be explained away using common sense and logic. One such case I'll never forget happened while I was visiting a Spiritualist church in England back in 1998.

I'd just finished my demonstration of mediumship at around 8 P.M., when the president of the church asked if I'd help him with an elderly lady. She claimed to be having a terrible time with a spirit who was haunting her house and frightening her during the night. Since she lived just five minutes from the church, I thought, *Why not?*

When we arrived at the house, my mouth fell open at the sight that lay before me. The house looked as if a bomb had hit it. I thought, *This isn't poltergeists, it's terrorists!* However, I asked the woman about the phenomena she'd witnessed, and she began to walk me into a sitting room where the furniture was falling to pieces. It was here, she said, that she'd seen the front of her sideboard fall off one day while she was having tea. She claimed that it was her dead husband trying to make contact with her.

Next she took me to the kitchen, where there was an old boiler beside an open window. That boiler, she said, would go out regularly . . . so I closed the window and sorted that "ghost" out. Then she said that the spirit had taken her husband's false teeth and other objects from her bathroom. It was at this point that I looked more closely at her mouth and realized that her husband might be closer to her than she knew, as the bottom denture she was wearing was continually popping out of the right side of her mouth.

Finally, she led the church president and me upstairs to the bedroom where she heard the sounds and voices of the spirits who kept her awake at night. I must admit that upon entering the bedroom there *were* muffled noises from above the ceiling.

"Can you hear the voices?" she asked. What I *could* hear was the scratching and cooing of a bunch of pigeons in the attic. Now, I don't know if it was the mischievous side of my nature that overtook me then, but I gave the old lady a ritual that would expel the sounds in her room whenever she felt disturbed by them. I stood in the center of the room and clapped my hands together with as much force as I could. Almighty thunder could be heard from above, followed by silence. I was going to follow this with the line from the movie *Poltergeist,* when the medium, after ridding the family of the earthbound spirits, calls out, "This house is clean!" but that would have been taking it too far.

As we left, I couldn't help but think that there are more haunted people in the world than houses.

HAUNTED PEOPLE

Even though many buildings and places can give off an eerie feeling, and I'm sure that many old houses and castles hold memories of their previous inhabitants' lives, loves, hate, passion, and anger, I know through the work I do that images of the past can only be accessed if the right conditions are present. It leaves me thinking that there's no such thing as a haunted place unless you have a living person involved. It's a bit like the old Zen koan: If a tree falls in a forest, does it make a sound if there's no one there to hear it?

It's my opinion that *people* are haunted, and most of the phenomena they claim to experience take place in their own minds. I've witnessed many people who have sensed an eerie presence in an old building and then carried it into realms of the ridiculous with their own imaginations. You only have to take certain psychics or mediums into an ancient castle and they start to visualize old soldiers, scenes of battle and murders, and so on. I feel that a good medium who assists in a case of haunting should try to bring some peace of mind to the people who feel that their lives are being disturbed by such things. The last thing they need is to be told about gruesome murders and horrible tortures.

If someone has an overactive imagination, who knows what they can dream up, especially if they feel that they need attention from others around them? Cases of poltergeist activity are very rare, but many people tell stories of invisible presences in their homes or unexplained noises or objects being thrown violently around, only for it all to stop when the team of investigators arrives. Over the years, it's become easier for me to tell the difference between a case of genuine paranormal activity and that of a person who needs attention and has invented a haunting to get it. But either way, something isn't right, and it needs to be made right, whether the haunting is in the house or in the person's mind.

MIND OVER PSYCHIC MATTER

A case that illustrates this perfectly is that of a middle-aged woman who came to our Spiritualist church for help. She claimed that a spirit was having sexual intercourse with her in her sleep and that when she awoke, she felt disgusted and violated. She'd lived by herself since her marriage had ended in divorce several years earlier, and she said that the phenomena had begun shortly after this. At first she only felt a presence lying beside her, but as time passed it would overpower her, and she'd black out. When she awoke, she'd discover bruising around her thighs.

Mrs. Primrose knew from the moment she heard

this story that this had nothing to do with spirits, but she went along to the woman's house with another medium from the church and spent some time trying to sense whether or not there were any malevolent spirits around. After much discussion, she asked the woman if she'd like to come to the church for spiritual healing—and she insisted that the woman speak to her family doctor about the bruises and tell him her story.

The healers in our church gave this lady a lot of attention, compassion, and much-needed friendship, and the doctor referred her to a counselor. No one encouraged the idea that a spirit was involved in what she'd been experiencing, but many people offered to pray for her. Within a month, the experiences stopped. Sometimes all that's needed is for the afflicted person to find friendship and to be cared for by others.

The spirit world seems to get a lot of bad press when it comes to spooky happenings around people in this world. I suppose that for some, it's easier to blame the unseen than to lay the blame at their own door.

OPENING THE DARK ROOMS

When I see people who are afraid of the unexplained, it bothers me because I know that there's nothing to fear. With all the different experiences I've had in what people would consider the frightening world of ghosts, spirits, and haunted places, what I find lies at the heart of such things is the fear that everyone has in the dark rooms of their minds—those little compartments that we push all our phobias into, in the hopes that we don't have to open the door on them ever again. In everyday life, we can forget about them, but when we feel alone or emotionally vulnerable, they float up to our conscious mind and remind us that we have issues to deal with and fears to face.

As part of my development as a medium, I've had to explore the dark rooms where terror hides, face it, and conquer it. This is why I'm unafraid of things that go bump in the night. I also don't fear dying or what comes after that. Part of my journey is about exorcising my own demons, realizing my weaknesses, accepting them, and letting them go. As long as I do this type of self-investigation, I'll never feel haunted in my home, my life, or my mind.

Anyone can rid themselves of their fears by illuminating them with the light of knowledge. Even when you're faced with episodes of paranormal activity that defy all logic, there's still no need to invite fear into your mind. And just remember that many events with no rational explanation are actually intriguing and miraculous.

Chapter Six

PUBLIC NON-REALITY

At the end of October 2001, my son Steven, who had just turned 17, went off to join the Royal Navy. He'd just started his first week of training at the HMS *Raleigh* in Cornwall when I underwent what was to become one of the strangest episodes of my adult life.

Every Sunday I walked my dog, Charlie, in the old cemetery near my home. The Sunday after Steven left for the Navy, my friend Jim and I walked Charlie together. Charlie is an English springer spaniel, the type of dog that likes to run wild through undergrowth and bushes, chasing anything that moves. This particular day, he disappeared for about five minutes before Jim and I began to call his name and whistle for him to come back to us. Instead of Charlie's usual response, which would be to come panting through the bushes carrying a stick or stone, we could hear him barking as if he were in some sort of distress.

Jim and I made our way toward the sound and found ourselves in a very old part of the cemetery, where I'd never been before. Charlie was sitting in front of an old headstone, barking repeatedly. As I got closer, I noticed the name on the headstone and was shocked by what I saw: the grave of one Gordon Smith, who was a writer, and his son, Steven Andrew Smith, who'd died at sea during World War I. Neither Jim nor I could believe the coincidence, even down to the "Andrew," which is my son's middle name. I must say it felt very strange to look at this old grave, even though it dated back almost 100 years.

Six weeks after going into the Royal Navy, Steven decided that he wanted to leave; he simply felt that it wasn't the life for him. I never mentioned the gravestone to him, nor did I go back to the old part of the cemetery. It wasn't until February 2004 that I happened to be walking through the cemetery with Jim and Charlie and we decided to walk back up to see the grave that had spooked us so much two and a half years earlier.

It was what we *didn't* see this time that was really spooky. The stone still read "Gordon Smith, Writer," but there was absolutely no mention of Steven Andrew—or, for that matter, any son at all. The only other name on the headstone was that of a daughter, Daphne, who had died in the 1920s. For the second time, Jim and I were staring at this stone, unable to believe what we were seeing. I could think of no way in which this old granite could have been physically changed in this way without some sign of deterioration or damage.

Had this happened to me when I was on my own, I would have put the whole episode down to my imagination, but the fact that my friend witnessed the same thing on both occasions made me wonder what was going on.

Who can explain such strange events? I simply call them *public non-reality,* a term for the supernatural episodes in life that may never be explained. I think of public non-reality whenever I come across cases in which more than one person has witnessed strange phenomena that defy our physical laws and have no rational explanation.

SPIRITS LIFTING

Albert Best was the sort of medium who never had to exaggerate his gifts—what he did tended to speak for itself. But when I was helping a friend research Best's life for a book, I did uncover an incredible example of public non-reality involving him. This account was given to me by a Catholic priest who lives just outside Glasgow.

I was invited, along with some friends of mine who had joined together to form an ecumenical group to study and discuss religious matters, to attend a session of mediumship given by the late Mr. Albert Best. The group met in Glasgow at the home of my friend who was hosting this session. I had been told by several members of the group who were familiar with the medium and his work that he could be quite phenomenal, but none of us could have ever expected what we were about to see.

Albert Best was a man small in stature, who appeared, in my view, very shy. He seemed to be intimidated by the gathering of men and women in our group who were of either of a religious or scientific background. Soon after the formal introductions, Mr. Best sat in a large and very heavy-looking armchair at the far end of the well-lit sitting room, while the rest of us were seated around the room in a sort of circle formation. Mr. Best closed his eyes and fell into a sort of trance, and a voice spoke through him in an accent that was hard to distinguish as any exact nationality. He began to give what I believe was a message from a spirit on the Other Side to one of my colleagues, who was confirming what he was hearing, when, without any warning, the chair on which Mr. Best was sitting began to shake furiously. Mr. Best snapped out of his trance state and began to protest to unseen forces around him, saying, "Stop that!" and "Put me down!"

If I had not been in the company of people whom I consider sane of mind, I would not have believed my eyes, as the chair, along with Mr. Best, lifted up till the little man's head was near ceiling height. No sooner had this happened than voices could be heard, which I can say came from no one seen sitting in that room. The chair slowly returned to the floor with Mr. Best still calling out to the invisible forces around him, and the session ended soon after. The medium explained that he was unharmed and never in any danger, but he did not like it when they played games like that just to impress people. He said that the spirits who had played this prank on him were men who had been part of his squadron during the war and who had died in Africa in 1943. This was Mr. Best's account; quite honestly, I, along with most of my group—even those among us with a background in physics—have absolutely no explanation for what we experienced.

Albert Best wasn't the only medium to levitate in the presence of such notable company. The most famous medium of the Victorian era, Daniel Douglas Home (pronounced *Hume*), was reported to have levitated many times. Many great men of science witnessed him floating in the air, while he made heavy items of furniture around him float at the same time. His feats of levitation happened not once, but hundreds of times in well-lit rooms.

Even though D. D. Home's amazing powers were tested in so many ways and by so many people, he was never seriously accused of fraud. He even astounded the physicist Sir William Crookes, who wrote favorably about Home's levitational abilities in *The Quarterly Journal of Science* in 1871. Crookes said that he couldn't conclude anything other than that the humanly impossible had happened.

D. D. Home's explanation for the phenomena

was the same as Albert Best's: that spirits he knew would lift and gently glide him around a room, never bringing harm to him or any other person concerned. The spirits, he'd say, were demonstrating their powers to convince people of a life beyond the physical one.

FLYER TUCK

Mediums aren't the only ones who have been seen to fly by members of the public. Joseph of Copertino, known in his lifetime as "the flying monk" and later St. Joseph, was seen in the air on many occasions. Joseph was born in Apulia, Italy, in 1603, and at the age of 21 became a Franciscan priest in the order of Conventuals near Copertino. He had a reputation for starving and flagellating himself so much that people soon thought of him as holy. One day during prayers and Mass in the chapel, he floated up over the other monks and landed gently on the altar in a state of ecstasy. Even though he flew directly over the many candles, he wasn't burned and his robes weren't singed. After many such episodes, he was sent to see the Pope in Rome. Once again, he floated off the ground and rose high into the air in a state of ecstasy.

Eventually, one of Joseph's superiors became very hostile toward him and decided to chastise and humiliate the monk; while under this superior, Joseph's flights stopped for almost two years. His ability to fly returned when he was allowed to visit Rome again, however. And when the people gave him an enthusiastic welcome, he flew more than 15 yards to embrace the statue of the Virgin Mary on the altar.

St. Joseph made no claim for a miraculous or divine reason to be airborne—all he needed, he said, was a feeling of deep joy. He'd experience these flights for the rest of his life, and even when he was close to death, his doctor reported that he was levitating six inches from his bed while he described the sounds and scents of Paradise waiting for him.

Joseph of Copertino was canonized just over 100 years after his death when the Pope ordered an investigation into his flights and found that they were backed up by hundreds of depositions. I don't know about anyone else, but I certainly think that to see a monk fly would be a good enough reason to attend church. But then again, the Lord does work in mysterious ways. . . .

THE NATURE OF MIRACLES

Who can say why certain miraculous events happen? And why don't we look more closely at the causes of such supernatural occurrences when they do happen? For years people have seen unbelievable happenings such as crying statues, apparitions of religious or holy figures, or even flying monks. Do we accept the miraculous only as long as it lies in the past and concerns gurus, saints, and messiahs? Are we afraid to see it as evidence of the fantastic nature of the human spirit?

We only have to look at the life of Jesus Christ: Do we actually believe that he walked on water, turned water into wine, or healed the sick—or are these seen as fables created to give us hope and faith? What about St. Bernadette's vision of the Virgin Mary at Lourdes, and the many other people who swear that they've witnessed such visions: Can they all be put down to imagination or self-delusion?

My own opinion is that all forms of public non-reality are caused by people, who, whether they're aware of it or not, are allowing more of their "super-conscious mind" to encroach on their earthly mind. This superconsciousness is the spiritual being, which emanates a small fraction of itself into human form, and in its more complete form, connects to the higher, more spiritual realms of life. It's only because people tend not to accept that they're much more than just people in the physical world that they find the supernatural hard to accept.

Miracles are no more than glimpses of other dimensions of the human consciousness, which, when they break into physical reality, distort our normal idea of life in such a way that we're faced with the unbelievable or unexplainable. This may change our view of reality and expand our consciousness. After all, weren't most of our religions founded by miraculous people who were teaching us about our spiritual nature?

The development of consciousness has allowed certain Buddhist monks, lamas, and yogis to practice feats of mind over matter, such as sitting in subzero temperatures but still producing enough body heat to dry a wet blanket within seconds. Others have been known to cover vast distances on foot in times that aren't humanly possible, while others have been seen in more than one location at the same time. This type of yogic practice has been going on for thousands of years, and even today there are many such yogis who can perform similar feats. How is this possible? It may be called "mind over matter," but what does that mean?

In order for there to be any form of miraculous event, there has to be a life form to instigate it. When visions appear to people, it's because they're allowing their own spiritual energy to be manipulated in order for the phenomena to occur, as most of these types of visions are projected through the mind of the person who experiences them. The same thing applies to most supernatural experiences.

TRUTHS AND MISCONCEPTIONS ABOUT
PUBLIC NON-REALITY

Myth #1: Miracles happen just because you want them to.

The truth is that even if you pray a lot, you're still not guaranteed anything.

Myth #2: If a famous saint or holy person has witnessed a miraculous vision at a certain site, you can, too.

No, it's not likely, even if you make a pilgrimage to the site itself.

Myth #3: Most people who cause supernatural phenomena to occur do so deliberately.

In fact, most don't know that they've done it at all, and very few such "miracle workers" could produce a repeat performance.

Myth #4: Superhuman beings can produce gifts from the higher realms out of thin air for their devotees.

This often just reeks of a scam to recruit new members to a cult.

Myth #5: Statues can cry tears from heaven.
Check the roof they're under for leaks!

Myth #6: The world is full of miracles.

It is, but most of them are natural phenomena.

FACES IN THE FLOOR

In the early '90s I was working as a medium in Spain, and I was hosted by Ray and June Smith, who were members of the Gibraltar Society for Psychical Research. On a day off, Ray asked if I'd like to look at a videotape of one of the more fascinating cases he'd investigated.

The film began with Ray entering a small house in Belmez, a Spanish village in the Sierra Nevada mountains. Inside he was introduced to a small elderly woman named Maria Gomez Pereira, who led him into her kitchen. As the video recorder was pointed at the floor, I was astonished to see many faces. I first thought that these had been painted or sketched by an artist, but it turns out that they'd been appearing on Maria Gomez Pereira's kitchen floor since 1971.

When the first face (a man's) appeared to Maria and her family, they decided to have the cement slab lifted and a new one laid in its place. In just two weeks, a second face had appeared in the same place as before. Again the family wanted to remove the slab; however, at this point the mayor of Belmez stepped in and had the slabs with faces preserved. It was decided that the floor should be excavated because there were stories that the house had been built on an old graveyard. Some human bones were found and were given a proper burial in the hopes that this would put an end to the strange episode. Once again a new cement floor was laid, only now more faces appeared—not only a man's this time, but also that of a woman and many other smaller faces of different people surrounding her.

By now Maria Gomez's house was attracting the attention of all sorts of investigators and scientists. Some even tested the cement floors that had previously been removed for signs of paints and charcoals, but none were found. One team of scientists left cameras recording over a period of weeks, and the film clearly showed that faces were appearing from the floor as if by magic. Some would come and stay, while others would come and go.

Ray's video shows many faces: men, women, and children of all ages and expressions. As I watched, I got the feeling that Maria was the cause of the phenomenon, that her emotions affected the expressions on the faces. It's my feeling that when people discover such things, they themselves have given emotional energy to the occurrences, and more often than not, they're responsible for the activity. If they're not around, nothing will happen.

The faces are still appearing on the floor of Maria's house, and I believe that they won't stop until Maria herself is no longer there. But, after more than 20 years, scientists and psychic researchers still haven't come any closer to finding an explanation for the faces in the floor.

MORE TO US THAN MEETS THE EYE

The unseen energy that flows around us has much more to do with public non-reality than we know. On one occasion I was giving a message from a man in the spirit world to his wife in a private sitting, when he told me to tell her that he always gave her a red rose on Valentine's Day. No sooner had I mentioned this to her than a red rose from a vase on her table lifted up by itself and landed on her lap. In her eyes this was some kind of miracle, but as a medium, I knew that the spirit of her husband had used my energy to do this, since during the transporting of the rose from one place to the other, I felt a dullness run through my body, as though someone had put their hand into my stomach and removed something. Energy had to be taken from me to allow the moving of the flower.

Supernatural events in this world are all created out of the energies in and around us. Even when a person sees an apparition, the spirit is using the person's energy in order to appear physical again.

This may explain the strange sensation people get at such times—quite apart from the shock of the whole episode, there's also a draw on the person's energy field. In cases where mediums are used to enable spirits to appear in a physical way, the medium will feel a pull on his or her own energy, just as I did when the rose was being transported. It's only because mediums are more acquainted with the more subtle energies than the average person that they don't consider the experience to be strange at all.

NOT ALL THERE

For years mediums have produced a physical phenomenon known as *materialization,* which allows the spirits to reproduce their own physical images by using the life force of the medium they're working with. This type of mediumship was at its height from Victorian times to World War II, and thousands of people saw their loved ones rematerialize at séances, where they were able to speak to them in person, as it were.

In order for this type of mediumship to take place, the medium would usually have to go into a very deep trance in which his or her bodily functions would slow to almost a standstill. This was required in order for the spirit to use the life energy of the medium to mold their own image and for a period of time come back into the physical dimension.

The effect on the medium was to be left depleted of energy after the séance. Even others sitting at the séance would feel drained, as physical energy would often be taken from some of them as well to sustain the materialization.

At one séance, the aunt of one young man came through and spoke to her relative for almost half an hour. It was only when she lifted the gown she appeared to be wearing that he realized she was only half materialized—from the waist up. She said that there wasn't enough energy to reproduce her entire body. Nonetheless, she told her nephew that since she'd just come to speak to him, she didn't require her legs to do so. At other séances, hands or just faces would appear, because the energy from the group and the medium combined wasn't strong enough to allow a full materialization to take place.

Over many years and through many mediums, thousands of people have witnessed spirits becoming solid forms and conversing with their loved ones, if only for a short time. There are thousands of testimonies, infrared photographs, and voice recordings, many of which have been authenticated by doctors, scientists, politicians, and others whom we'd have to consider to be of sane mind, not to mention the masses who saw and conversed with their loved ones, whom we'd think they'd recognize. Yet no matter how many times this type of manifestation has taken place, there have always been objections and claims of fraud and skulduggery from the skeptics. Some of these *have* been founded, although many other cases that were tried and tested and defied the law of physics have simply collected dust in files as unexplained mysteries. If nothing else, there was always a great deal of controversy going on in the old séance rooms, some of which even made headline news.

THE LAST WITCH

A medium who certainly made headlines in Britain back in 1944 was the famous materialization medium Helen Duncan. Her mediumship became the talk of the town after she gave a séance in Portsmouth in January 1944, when a young sailor materialized in solid form and spoke to his mother, telling her that he'd been killed when his ship, the HMS *Barham,* had been sunk. He went on to mention that a great many of his shipmates had been killed and were with him on the Other Side. He also told his mother that she wouldn't receive confirmation of his death from the War Office for another three weeks.

Can you imagine what it felt like for that mother to see her son appear to her in this way? So strong was her belief in what had happened at the séance that she immediately contacted the

Admiralty, asking them for conformation of the sinking of the *Barham*. She wasn't given it, but instead was visited by two senior officials who questioned her about the information she had on the sinking of the ship. She told them about the séance and then heard nothing more about the matter until three weeks later, when she was, as her son had told her, given confirmation of his death due to the sinking of his ship.

Meanwhile, at Helen Duncan's next séance, her spirit guide made an appearance and asked the people who were responsible for running the séances in the Portsmouth Spiritualist church to beware of naval officers attending future séances. He warned that they mustn't be allowed in or they'd bring great harm to his medium.

It would appear that no one at the church paid any attention to this warning because later that month, at a séance again held in the Portsmouth church, Helen had just gone into a state of trance and started emanating ectoplasm from her solar plexus when two naval officers and an undercover policeman suddenly jumped to their feet, put on the lights, and called out, "Police!"—at which point, the door was kicked in by other police officers who made a grab for the ectoplasm, saying that it was actually cotton sheets.

Before going into a trance, Helen Duncan always insisted on being searched by members of the group to rule out any fraud. She'd also strip down to her underwear and put on a thin robe, which anyone could examine before she began to work. After that, no one would interfere with her in any way, as to do so when she was in a trance could be very damaging to her. So when the police seized her, she came out of the trance in a terrible state, and no one who was attending the séance could help her. Helen's body was badly burned around the stomach and solar plexus, and she was in a state of shock as she and the leaders of the church were arrested and taken into police custody.

Helen was kept in prison for three months without any chance of bail until her trial, which was held at the Old Bailey in London in April 1944. At that infamous courthouse, she was tried under the Witchcraft Act of 1735, and unbelievably, sentenced to nine months in Holloway prison for demonstrating her mediumship—even though there was no evidence that she had cheated. The people attending the séance had asked to be thoroughly searched, but inexplicably, the police refused. To this day, no one can understand why Helen was held in prison for such a long time without any chance of bail. It seems to me that someone wanted her out of the way so that she wouldn't give the public any more official war secrets.

Medium Rare

The kind of phenomena produced by mediums such as Helen Duncan and many other amazing mediums of the past must have been the most convincing evidence that there was truly a life after death. The sad reality about that type of mediumship was that it lent itself to fraud, and I'm sure that many people did fake séances to make money off of the bereaved.

I never got to see Helen Duncan's mediumship, as she died in 1956, but my old teacher, Mrs. Primrose, once gave me a fascinating account of one of the many times she witnessed Helen's amazing gifts.

Mrs. P. told me how she and a friend helped to search Helen before the séance, and that all she was wearing was a pair of underwear under a flimsy black robe. After the search, the medium was taken to a seat (where her hands and feet were bound) that was placed behind a black curtain at the corner of the séance room. All the lights were switched off, and a dim red light was set in front of the black curtain; minutes later, a white mist could be seen by the entire group of 16 people sitting in the seats in a circle around the room. This ectoplasm grew thicker and began to take the form of a man who stood about six feet tall (which was much taller than Helen). He spoke to the group, telling them that his name was Albert—he was Helen's guide and would help bring through the spirits who wanted to communicate.

Mrs. Primrose described how ten different spirits materialized one after the other—all of whom were recognized by their families and friends. One little girl of about four years of age ran to her mother and hugged her, saying that she was all right now and that her mom shouldn't cry anymore. Mrs. P. also had a message at that séance from one of her old neighbors, who asked her to pass on some information to her husband, whom she said Mrs. P. would meet the following day. She asked her not to be shocked when she met him, as he'd had his right leg amputated since she last saw him.

At the close of the séance, Helen was untied and allowed to dress. Next, she came and spoke to the group, asking them if they'd received any good messages, as she'd been in such a deep trance that she had no recollection of the proceedings.

Mrs. Primrose was a medium herself, and a person who I'm certain would be able to detect fraud in a second. In this case, she felt sure that the incredible phenomena were quite genuine. The following evening, in her own church, she saw the husband of the spirit neighbor who had asked her to pass on the message. He was sitting in the back row of the church, and as Mrs. P. went toward him, he stood up to greet her, saying, "It's been a long time, Jean." She said that her mouth fell open when she realized that, just as his wife had said, his right leg was missing. This was further proof, not that she needed it, after witnessing the full materialization of ten spirit people the previous evening.

Both during and after her life, Helen Duncan was the subject of many investigations, with a variety of conclusions being drawn about her mediumship. A number of books have been written about her, some of which are listed in the Further Reading section, and anyone interested in her life should have no trouble finding additional information.

UNBELIEVABLE BUT TRUE

Many people have claimed to have witnessed miracles and other extraordinary events that defy natural laws as we understand them. There are numerous accounts of physical phenomena and miraculous occurrences of public non-reality held in the Society for Psychical Research in London and other bodies and religious groups around the world, filed under "Unexplained." Even though there's often no accounting for certain cases, this doesn't mean that the events haven't occurred, only that there's no rational explanation for them. As a medium, I encounter many people who tell me about episodes of public non-reality, yet I'm never shocked or surprised by them. Even the more unbelievable may turn out to be true and have meaning.

It's all too easy to dismiss such claims, but we can often see their effects in the lives of the people affected. Episodes of public non-reality will often cause the witnesses to rethink their lives and expand their consciousness in a spiritual way. They can tear down the boundaries of the mind and broaden the horizons, bringing an awareness of the true power of consciousness. When our conscious mind is ready to accommodate supernatural occurrences, then the so-called miraculous will be considered the norm.

Chapter Seven

ALTERED STATES

I was 11 years old and traveling on a train with my parents and two of my older brothers when I first experienced something very strange. We'd been in London to visit my mother's brother, Mick, for Easter and were on our homeward journey, which at that time took eight hours. It was going to be a very long day.

I'd been given a new watch by Uncle Mick that had kept me quiet for a while (except for my telling everyone that another minute had passed). My brothers seemed to spend their time better than I did—they read and drew, only interrupting my parents' conversation now and then to ask, "How long to go?"

I'd become fascinated by the second hand on my watch and was transfixed as I watched it go around. I became aware of the light in the compartment changing from its usual yellowy-whitish glow to a very dull, almost sepia color; meanwhile, the smoke from my mother's cigarette was turning from a silvery mist into an amazing orange color, and my family began to look like negatives of themselves. My head was down, looking at my wrist on the small table just under the large window, but somehow I was also standing in a room that was familiar to me, watching my best friend, Alex (who lived next door to me in Glasgow). Alex was standing over a bed where his mother lay looking very sick indeed, and I could hear her say, "That's enough now." The boy was then led out of the room by someone taller than he was.

In the compartment of the train, my mother was asking me what I was looking at and was forcing me to answer her, my brothers were making up funny songs, and my father was half asleep with his head hanging to one side. Yet I could still see Alex, who was holding a large Easter egg in his hands— only now he was in a dim sepia-colored light, and his father was telling him not to cry.

"What are you staring at?!" my mother shouted.

"My watch," I answered slowly. "It's six o'clock." We were halfway through our journey.

I was now totally back with my family on the train, and soon I fell asleep. I remember my father waking me just after 10 P.M. to tell me that we'd arrived in Glasgow. I slept again on the short ride from the train station to our house and was put to bed by my father.

The following morning I wanted to go next door to Alex's house with a gift I'd bought him in London, but my mother explained that Alex's mother had died, and I should wait until another time to give him his gift.

I saw Alex just after his mother's funeral, and he told me that he'd seen her just before she died—when she'd given him an Easter egg that he'd keep forever. I asked him what time she'd died, and he said he didn't know exactly, but he'd seen her at six o'clock. He knew this because his sister, who had been asked to look after him, had arrived just before six.

Looking back at this experience, I can see a similarity to what's known as *remote viewing,* where a psychic can be in one place and focus his or her mind on an event taking place somewhere else (distance doesn't limit this type of psychic vision). I can also liken it to *astral travel,* where the mind can be projected to other places and bring back information. In both remote viewing and astral projection, a person can hone his or her skill to choose where he or she wishes to go.

For me this was the beginning of what I now know to be trance mediumship, where my mind "moves out" to allow spirit beings to use it and my body to communicate with their loved ones.

The Meditative Mind

I'm sure that many people would say I'm not in possession of my full mind anyway, especially when I try to describe some of my early experiences. In fact, from a young age, I tried to dismiss some of the more bizarre events myself, putting them down to childish fantasies and daydreams—I even wondered if I'd made them up to get attention. Nevertheless, most of what had happened to me contained information that was intelligent, true, and beyond my knowledge.

I very rarely mentioned my experiences at all after the reaction I got from my mother the first time I saw a materialized spirit and had an intelligent conversation with him. All I can say is that she sent me out of the house in a hurry. It was only when I joined a spiritual-development class in my 20s that I began to make sense of what was really happening to me in my childhood. A big part of my development was to clear my mind through meditation, to look at myself and my life in a rational and fully focused way, and to try to understand my mind.

❀ ❀ ❀

The reason that we mediums have to learn to understand our own minds is so we can distinguish the difference between our own thoughts and any telepathic communications or psychic images from another source. Meditation helps ground us, and practicing it on a regular basis enables us to be more in control of how we think. It assists us in controlling our actions and shaping our attitudes in a much better way.

Even though I started out as a good meditator and had no problem focusing my mind, grounding myself in reality, and breathing well, I began to notice now and then that when my mind became clear and still, either with my eyes closed or open, I'd experience a change of light and tone around me. Often when this would occur, I'd sense my awareness separating into two parts. While being able to stay in the moment, I'd find that I was equally aware of being somewhere else—and I could describe both situations in full detail.

My teacher, Mrs. Primrose, never saw this as a problem; in fact, she often commented that I was a natural medium and that this type of thing would happen from time to time. She told me to keep a record to see if there appeared to be a pattern to this separating of consciousness. I was to note the time frame I found myself in and check out, where possible, if the scenes I was observing could be validated by anyone else.

Mrs. P. told me that I was what's known as a *trance medium,* and that not only could I receive messages in my mind from the Other Side (also called *mental mediumship*), but I could also enter a trance and allow my mind and body to be used by a spirit person for more direct communication. She told me that I'd have to learn to control this sort of mediumship, or if I didn't wish to be used in this way, I'd have to learn to close down this area of my mind and focus solely on my mental mediumship.

I decided to learn more about trance mediumship.

COMING THROUGH

One of the greatest trance mediums was the man who became a great friend and mentor to me, Albert Best. Albert was very understated about what he did, but when I was working for the Gibraltar Society for Psychical Research, I found a videotape of him carrying out spiritual healing on a woman who had a large, painful lump protruding from her neck. Albert, in a trance, could be seen standing beside the woman with his hands about an inch from her body, moving them slowly over her neck area. A moment later, a voice came through him in a foreign language. The woman responded in the same language, but with a look of surprise on her face. The unbelievable thing about this was that the language was Mandarin. Seconds later—again, unbelievably—the lump disappeared completely. The patient was reduced to tears of joy, while Albert shook his head, opened his eyes, lit a cigarette, and chatted in English to the psychic researchers who were monitoring the situation as if nothing unusual had happened.

I later asked Albert about this episode and how he was able to speak in another language. He explained that whenever he gave a healing, a spirit guide would come through him, or "overshadow" him, which meant that Albert's conscious mind was displaced. Thus, the spirit guide could work through Albert, enabling the spirit performing the healing to have better use of his body. And when the patient understood the guide's own language, he could use Albert's voice to speak as he would have when alive in the physical world.

Incidentally, Mr. Best normally spoke in an accent that was a mixture of Glaswegian and his native Irish, which made it difficult for people to understand his English, let alone a foreign language!

MIND CONTROL

What Albert had been practicing in this case was a variation of controlled trance mediumship, in which the spirit guide of the entranced medium uses the medium's voice to pass messages from the spirit world, rather than sending mental images through the medium's mind.

One of the mediums Albert looked up to as a great exponent of controlled trance was Helen Hughes, whose work during World War II was revered by Spiritualists, and who had a huge public following in Britain and other countries. Sometimes as many as 2,000 people would pack halls around the UK to witness Mrs. Hughes demonstrate her amazing gift.

Like Albert Best, Helen Hughes was known for her public mediumship more than her trance mediumship, but those who experienced this amazing medium in an altered state became convinced that spirit people were actually controlling her voice. Many people who witnessed her work also testified that the spirit person who was speaking through her would often be seen transfiguring her face.

I spoke to a lady from India who'd had a sitting with Helen Hughes while visiting the UK back in the early 60s. It wasn't something that this woman had planned, and she hadn't even been interested in the subject of life after death when she'd been introduced to Helen; nevertheless, the woman asked the medium if she'd try to make contact with the Other Side for her. The private sitting was recorded, and as I listened to it, I thought of how much I still had to learn to reach the level of mediumship demonstrated by Helen Hughes or Albert Best.

On the tape, Helen begins talking normally, explaining what might or might not happen during the sitting, and the Indian woman can be heard answering politely. Then Helen claims to make contact with the woman's grandmother in the spirit world, and within a short amount of time, she's speaking in a completely different voice: one of the Indian languages.

Even now, the sitter can't believe what happened. The details given could only have come from her grandmother, who'd died some years earlier. Helen had even used a pet name that her grandmother alone had used for her as a child.

As a result of this sitting, Helen Hughes was invited to work in India. There are a great many reports and taped evidence from her time there to prove that on many occasions she channeled the spirits of Indian people who spoke through her in their own native tongue. Helen herself was never, to anyone's knowledge, able to speak any foreign language.

Out of My Mind

As I progressed in my development group, I began to notice the different stages of trance. My conscious mind separating to be in two places at once was only the beginning. Once I learned to accept that this was a way to intensify my abilities as a medium, I relaxed and allowed the spirit who had been one of my guides from my early childhood to take me through each step as it came to me. Mrs. Primrose was always there to give me answers when I was unsure, and by now I'd also become friendly with Albert Best, who also took an interest in how my mediumship was progressing.

It was around this time that I experienced my first deep trance, during which I was controlled by a spirit person who wanted to communicate with Mrs. P. The feeling was so overwhelming that I don't really recall what happened, but my wonderful teacher later told me that the information given through me might help someone she knew who was in a lot of trouble. I can see now that this message was so important that any interference from my mind might have distorted it, so the spirit person decided to put me into a state of deep trance. Although I remembered nothing of what happened, the experience felt so amazing that I wanted to learn more about it.

Soon I was able to stay alert and feel each change my body and mind went through in order to allow my spirit guide to forge a strong link with me. First I'd feel my mind expanding in a way that allowed me to be aware of what was happening around me, as well as what was happening to others who were sitting nearby. Then I'd feel a pulse or rhythmic vibration in the room itself, as if all the empty space between every person or object was alive and breathing. There were times I could even hear people thinking—at this point, my body would feel as if it were shutting down, organ by organ, until all I was aware of was my heart beating more and more slowly, like a metronome slowing to an almost complete stop. This was the point at which I blacked out the first time I went through this experience, but when I learned to go beyond this sensation, I could actually feel the spirit people around me. They seemed more physical to me than the people who were alive and well in the room with me.

It took me years to allow my mind to open up to this level, even though I was a natural-born medium. Every time I sat in my group, I'd learn to let go a little bit more and clear out more of the emotional garbage that I'd allowed to clutter my mind for years, which can distort spirit communication. Part of the discipline of development is to learn not to become affected emotionally, but to remain still when all there is in the mind is motion.

There came a point when I could sit in this state and speak clearly to the spirit people the way I'd done as a child, before my mind had been conditioned by fear and emotional pain. Now I knew for sure that I was able to move out of my emotional mind and experience my own spirit linking and conversing with others for a short while. During this time I'd feel the presence of my spirit guide moving closer to me, until I was engulfed by the warm, loving sensation of being held in a beautiful state of grace by a highly evolved being of light.

It was when my consciousness had moved away and my guide had filled the space that was left that he'd use my voice to speak to the other people in the room, often giving them messages from spirit people they'd lost, or speaking to them directly and answering any questions they had about the afterlife. He said that he'd lived many years ago in China, that he was a man of no great importance, and that any wisdom he'd garnered came from observing nature. My guide said that his intention was to help people understand compassion and lose their fear of living. (It's often said that with spirit guides and their mediums, like attracts like, but I think he made a mistake in choosing me to work through!)

The more I practiced this type of trance mediumship, the stronger my own abilities as a mental medium became. Now when I work in public I have a sense of my guide slightly overshadowing me. Nothing has convinced me more that we're spirit and live far past this physical realm than the experience of being beyond my own mind in a state of trance, where the spirit people are so real that I can touch them. It's this understanding that has given me trust in what I do.

TRUTHS AND MISCONCEPTIONS
ABOUT TRANCE

Myth #1: Mediums who go into a trance make moaning sounds and gyrate their bodies in circles before speaking in a loud, exaggerated voice.

Yes, they do . . . when they're hamming it up!

Myth #2: Trance mediums sit in darkened rooms by candlelight listening to whale sounds on a tape recorder.

They can—but it doesn't help!

Myth #3: Spirit guides speak through trance mediums to spout hellfire and brimstone or to predict the end of the world.

There's normally a good reason why spirit guides have made the effort to communicate through a medium, but it's usually not to deliver apocalyptic messages.

Myth #4: A real experience of trance will leave the medium exhausted.

This shouldn't be the case; instead, it should fill the medium with spiritual energy and vitality. They should be radiant at the end of it.

Myth #5: Cleopatra, Jesus Christ, and other well-known figures pop in regularly to communicate.

This is usually just wishful thinking on the part of the so-called medium.

Myth #6: All you need to do to go into a trance is to close your eyes and speak in a different voice.

This just isn't true—use your common sense to assess what you've heard and the reason why it was said. And don't believe everything you hear!

BIG WOMAN, DEEP TRANCE

The funny thing about a medium going into a trance and speaking in a different voice is that it *is* funny. (I mean funny peculiar, not funny ha-ha.) One story especially comes to mind here, which I always share with students who wish to learn about deep trance mediumship.

Back in Glasgow in the late '60s, a woman I'll call Joan for the purposes of this story went along to a Spiritualist church. She'd become interested in the subject and felt that she was a bit psychic herself, yet she was quite surprised to receive a message from the medium on her first visit. The medium told Joan that she was indeed psychic and should learn to develop her gift in a development class. After the service finished, she gave Joan the name and address of a woman she should see to develop her gift.

Joan arrived at the address the following Thursday evening. Standing outside the front door, she felt a little apprehensive, but eventually she knocked on the door, which opened almost at once. There stood a very frail-looking elderly woman whom Joan thought must be the medium who would train her; instead, the little lady told her that she was only there to make tea for all of the people who sat together in the group. She then showed Joan into the front room of the house.

About ten people were sitting in a circular formation, and there was one empty chair, which Joan was directed toward by a very large lady who called out, "Ah, you must be Joan. Come and sit by me, and when we're all ready, we shall begin to meditate."

Joan sat down and wondered, *How do I do that?* No one explained what to do, and she was too scared to ask, so she just closed her eyes and thought about anything she could for the next half hour.

Finally, the roundly built woman beside her called out in a loud voice, "Stop and tell me what you witnessed during your meditation."

Joan panicked because she'd only thought about things that she had to do at home—but as she listened to some of the rubbish being spoken around the group, she decided to copy them and say that she was off on a spiritual journey.

"Now, Joan, tell me what happened to you," demanded the big lady.

"I saw an Indian gentleman dressed in lots of feathers," Joan lied.

"An Indian in feathers! Well, I shall expect great things from you in the future," the woman boomed. She then explained to the group that she was about to go into a very deep trance, and she required everyone to be completely silent since she could be injured or even killed if any member of the group moved or made a sound.

Joan sat holding her breath as she watched the large lady gyrate and wobble. With the weird sounds she was making, it seemed as though she were having a fit. Then, without warning, the woman jumped to her feet with her hands outstretched, and she started to speak in a very forced, deep voice. "Welcome, earthlings! I come from the planet Uranus, and I am here to give you advice about your planet."

Joan's eyes almost popped out of their sockets. Then, at that very moment, this gem of trance philosophy was interrupted by the door opening slowly. For a moment Joan was afraid of what might be coming in, but it turned out to be the old tea lady, who paid no attention to the woman in the trance and went around the circle of people asking what they'd like on their sandwiches. Joan watched her make her way around the group, until she stopped behind the medium and whispered, "What would you like on your sandwiches: cheese or ham?"

As quick as a flash, the big lady's head turned and she broke her trance for a second. "Ham!" she shouted loudly, and then went immediately back to giving the "earthlings" a dressing-down for ruining their planet!

For some reason, Joan never went back to that development group after that night.

A FAMOUS TRANCE

That message from Uranus might not have had much of an impact on the world, but during that same period of the "swinging '60s," what happened to a medium from London did. Ena Twigg caused a sensation when it became public knowledge that James Pike, an American bishop, had visited her to make contact with his son, Jim.

Jim had died a tragic death: After experimenting with psychedelic drugs in San Francisco, he'd shot himself in a New York hotel room in February 1966. Not long after his death, Bishop Pike and others close to him had begun to experience poltergeist activity in the apartments the bishop shared with his chaplain and secretary. Soon after this, the bishop learned of Ena Twigg's reputation as a medium, and at their first meeting she fell into a trance and began to converse with him in the voice of his son. Young Jim spoke openly to his father about his life and death, and he accepted responsibility for the poltergeist activities, explaining that he'd needed to get his father's attention.

For whatever reason, spirits who communicate in this way seem to be able to describe certain events in the future—likewise, Jim Pike told his father that he'd be with him when he was in Virginia, which would be very soon. The bishop knew nothing of any trip to Virginia . . . however, on his way home his plane was rerouted and landed at Dulles airport, which is on the Virginia side of Washington, D.C.

The bishop became convinced that Mrs. Twigg's mediumship was genuine. As he said in his book, *The Other Side,* there were too many exact references to episodes in his son's life, and there was no way that the medium could have known so much about that life or reproduced his son's characteristics in her state of trance.

But this wasn't the end of the Bishop Pike case for Ena Twigg. In August 1969, the bishop and his wife, Diane, were on vacation in the Israeli wilderness when they became lost and exhausted. The bishop rested in a cave in the desert, while his wife went for help. She was able to reach civilization, but the rescue party couldn't find the cave she described—it wasn't until September 4 that the bishop was finally found, dead.

Three days earlier, while sitting in her home in Acton, London, Ena Twigg had felt that she needed to sit with her husband and friends in a séance. The moment she went into a trance, the bishop came through, described exactly where his body lay, and gave certain messages that were to be passed on to his wife. Later, Diane Pike wrote in an article that the medium had given her details regarding her husband and the ordeal they'd both come through that no one else could have known. There were also many references to personal things shared only by the couple.

In Ena Twigg's own book, *The Woman Who Shocked the World,* she describes the situation from her point of view, and claims that the spirit of the bishop was around her for days after he'd gone missing. When no one had found his body, she decided to allow him to come through her and communicate his whereabouts for the sake of his poor wife.

LIGHTNESS OF MIND

No matter what you read or hear about people who make extraordinary claims about trances, there's nothing better than to witness them in action. While I was learning about mediumship in my development class, I met many interesting trance mediums, some of whom were totally deluded. One man who attended the group for a short time was more of a mediumistic impressionist than a trance medium, as he'd go through a repertoire of phony guides from John the Baptist through most of the 12 apostles to a highly exaggerated Jewish-sounding Jesus. After a while, Mrs. Primrose gave him his marching orders. (Strangely enough, she chose Good Friday to do so.)

To experience the worst side of mediumship only makes you appreciate the real thing even more. I'm sure that deluded mediums such as the man of the many biblical voices produce this nonsense only to gain attention or feel special in some way—luckily, in his case, no one else was harmed by his charade. However, gullible or vulnerable people have been taken in by mediums who claim to channel famous spirit guides, and this just isn't acceptable.

Once, a man from the south of England also claimed to be the medium for Jesus, and several women in the church he practiced in would sit around the so-called master and listen to his wise words, only to find that the alleged spirit was trying to get them all into bed. Most of these women saw through the ridiculous act of manipulation, but one of them fell for it and eventually left her husband for the "sleeping prophet," and the divorce cost her innocent husband a great deal of money, his home, and much heartache. I say this to remind people that for every genuine medium out there, there's going to be someone who's just out for all he or she can get.

The real experience of sitting with a trance medium will lift you to a more spiritual level and create a feeling of lightness of mind. There's a sort of sharing between the spirit world and this one that's difficult to put into words, but can definitely be felt by all who attend such a session.

� ✕ ✕

Of all of the mediums I've witnessed in a trance state, one sticks in my memory: She was someone who allowed me to experience a spiritual state of mind that will stay with me as long as I live. Her name was Laura, and she was the best trance medium I've ever witnessed.

Although by now I was experiencing short episodes of trance in my development class, Laura helped me understand the sequence my mind would go through to be raised from human consciousness to a heightened awareness of the spiritual realities. First, I learned to clear my mind and just allow any thoughts to pass through without attaching any importance to them; then I'd focus on relaxing my body. At this point, I'd become aware of how heavy my body had become and how slow and steady my breathing was.

By stilling my body and not allowing my mind to hold any mundane or material thoughts, I'd feel a sense of lightness of mind, which would expand as if I were the aura that surrounded my body. My physical limitations no longer applied, and I could open my mind to the idea of making a connection with the higher spirit who was waiting to link with me. It was as if I had to learn to go halfway to meet the spirits, but by doing so, I could sense more about them and train my mind to hold this connection for longer periods each time.

Also, I'd reached a point where my rational mind wouldn't limit me by dissecting and doubting what I was experiencing. From this state of consciousness, I could see, hear, and feel spirit people just as I'd done in childhood—and with the same trust I'd had as a young boy.

Being in an altered state of consciousness such as this is like being in a body of light, which feels limitless—time and space have no meaning. When you have to come back to current reality, it feels like coming back through clouds of mist that become denser and thicker until you feel totally connected to the physical world again. I've often thought that if this is anything close to the sensations the spirit goes through when the physical body dies, then what on earth is there to fear?

FROM DARKNESS COMES LIGHT

Now I have absolutely no problem with this type of enlightened experience, for I've trained my mind to cope with such things for the past 15 years, and I have an understanding of how it works and will benefit others. When I was a child, however, such experiences would happen completely at random.

I go back to when I was 16 years old and sitting with my friend Alex in his bedroom. We were with another boy who hung around with us at the time, listening to records and talking generally about nothing of any great importance, when I began to feel as if my body were vibrating. Even though we were teenagers, we weren't smoking anything funny or drinking alcohol. I have to say I had no wish to have a weird trip or experience any form of paranormal activity—what was about to happen couldn't have been further from my mind.

I looked at my two friends, who were sitting cross-legged on the floor opposite me, and I noticed that they were becoming darker, yet the room around them was becoming brighter. There was a cold feeling coming up from the floor, and I began to sense that my friends were staring at me. The whites of their eyes were almost luminous, but their faces had almost vanished into a cloud of darkness.

Alex broke the silence that had fallen over the room by asking if anyone else felt strange. The other boy said he was scared, and asked, "What's going on? Everything's gotten dark."

The vibrating around me had now grown to such a pitch that my body felt as if it were being shaken; then from out of nowhere, a voice came from my mouth and told Alex, "I am always with you. Remember, I am always with you, no matter what." My head was filled with a rushing sound, and in a second the room was back to normal.

The three of us just stared at each other. Alex was looking directly at my face, and I noticed that he was breathing really fast. The other boy asked what had gone on, told me I was freaky, and got up and left in a hurry. Alex quietly told me that he'd seen his mother looking at him and speaking to him through my face. Knowing that his mother was dead, I began to feel that I'd done something wrong, even though I hadn't intended to. I remembered the way my mother would react if I mentioned people that I'd seen who were dead. Alex told me not to feel bad about it because he was all right, and the more he thought about it, the more he smiled.

We sat together for hours that night, and I told my friend about some of the strange things that had happened to me. I shared how people had always said that my experiences were wrong, even though I had no idea how to make them happen or even how to make them stop. Alex was fascinated, and I felt relieved that I'd told him about my bizarre psychic escapades, although when it was time for me to go home, I asked him not to tell anyone about what had happened or about the things I'd mentioned to him.

Sometime in my 20s I lost touch with Alex, as our lives went in different directions. I never thought about that strange episode in his house again until one day when I was at work in a barber shop in Glasgow. To my surprise, the boy who had fled the scene so many years ago came in for a haircut. Now in his 30s (as was I), he asked me if I'd heard about Alex. I had no idea what he was talking about, so he told me that our old mutual friend had died from a long illness the previous week.

After the initial shock, I remembered the message from Alex's mother and how happy he'd been with the knowledge that no matter what, she'd always be with him. I look back now and am glad that her message came through, even if I had to experience some strange, altered state of consciousness for it to happen. I'm sure that when Alex was lying very ill, knowing that he was going to die, he would have taken comfort in the fact that his mother was waiting for him on the Other Side, no matter what.

"WHEN ALL AROUND YOU IS IN MOTION . . ."

Learning about trance mediumship and the process of altering your own state of consciousness to accommodate it is important for any medium. It gives you a much deeper awareness of the mechanics behind the gift.

Furthermore, the knowledge you gain about yourself and the workings of the human mind also assist you when you're practicing on people who come to you in a very emotional state. Mediums should know how to still their own minds, no matter how emotional the situation they find themselves in, and this should be made easier by what they've learned in their development about calming themselves and working through their mental problems. It's a bit like emptying out cupboards where we've hung on to stuff that we'll probably never use again; only in the mind, it's about remembering, accepting, and then letting go of what's there.

If a medium is working from a clear mind, this should help calm the sitter as well as further the process of giving spirit messages. The aim is to allow the spirit to come through in such a way that the sitter's mind will be raised in its vibration to the level of the medium's mind, which will allow the sitter to feel the spirit energy as well as be given proof of life after death. In a sense, a sitting with a trance medium should alter the state of mind of the sitter enough for him or her to experience a more complete feeling of his or her loved one. As I often tell people: "Feeling is believing."

Having gone through such a long training in mediumship, I've not only come to know that there's a spirit world where we'll go after physical death, but I've also developed my own awareness in the here-and-now. How I react to situations in my own life has changed somewhat, as instead of reacting emotionally to events that would have at one time upset me, I'm now able to approach life with a greater level of calmness and acceptance.

Our minds are almost always overactive with worry and fear, along with judgments of people and situations that we have no power over. Such thoughts can cause physical unrest or even illness. One of my spirit teachers would always say, "When all around you is in motion, be still in your mind and calm the motion."

This is something I hope I've learned to do for myself, and maybe even for others, too. To look at a situation with a calmness of mind usually allows you to see beyond the emotional extremes and realize the underlying cause, which in turn allows you to deal with it in a much more constructive way.

Chapter Eight

STRANDS OF TIME

As a teenager I often had what I now know were prophetic dreams and visions that showed me what was about to unfold in my own life or in that of one of my family members or friends. These dreams didn't really mean much to me, as they often involved simple things such as letters arriving that no one expected or surprising visits from family members and so on. These visions would occur when I was waking up—they were the sort of half-awake dreams that people remember having—or daydreaming, when my mind was drifting (normally during math lessons at school). I got to know the difference between ordinary dreams or daydreams and the prophetic kind, as the latter were always accompanied by a buzzing sound in my head that ended in a pop, which would snap me out of my contemplative state.

One sunny Saturday afternoon when I was about ten years old, I was playing with some friends at the back of our house when I suddenly became still and fixed my eyes on the brick wall that ran the length of the lane at the back of the houses on our street. I could hear a breathing sound around my head, which became a sort of hum, and I felt that I was in a different place but still looking ahead at a brick wall— but a much higher one this time. There was a group of people gathered at the foot of this wall, and they were all looking up at a young man hanging by one hand and screaming as if he were in pain. Then a fire engine arrived, and I could see my father talking with some of the firefighters. In a flash, the scene changed, and I felt that I was moving down a corridor in a hospital, where a doctor was standing with my older brother. I heard a popping noise, and my ears were full of the sounds of my friends playing in the back garden once again. Once the vision was over, I immediately went back to playing.

The following day I remember that there were lots of children hanging out in our street and quite a bit of accompanying shouting, screaming, and laughter. In the middle of all this hubbub, I saw a man running toward our home, and I remember watching him knocking on the door. My father came out, and I could see the man speaking quickly to him and urging him to go somewhere with him. Both men left in a hurry, and my father was gone for hours. He eventually returned with my older brother, whose right arm was in a plaster cast.

My brother had been climbing a wall about 30 feet high, looking for birds' eggs. He'd put his hand into the hole at the top of the wall where the nest was, and his foot had slipped and he'd fallen—but his wrist had been trapped, so he'd been left hanging on the wall. A woman had called for the fire department to help him and sent her husband to fetch my father, who said that by the time he arrived, there was a crowd of people looking up at his son dangling by his hand from the top of a very high wall. Luckily, my brother escaped with no more than a broken wrist, which was set when my father rushed him to the hospital.

Visions such as these occurred throughout my childhood; sometimes I'd tell people about them, but more often than not I'd keep them to myself because of the strange reaction I got from people. By the time I'd reached my 20s, I just accepted that every now and then I'd have one of my "funny turns." I had no idea what caused them or what to do about them, although I thought that if I could only learn how to work them to my advantage, then maybe I could see the outcome of the next race down at the track. Of course, now I know it doesn't work like that!

A Collage of Dreams

One of the more bizarre dreams I've had was when I was about 23 and working as a hairstylist. That particular cold winter's morning, I woke early but decided that I'd stay in bed as long as I could before getting up to face the world. My mind became fuzzy, and I drifted into that nice state somewhere between sleep and waking. Then I began to hear a soft pulsing sound like gentle breathing in my ears, which then built up to a buzzing sound. At the same time, pictures began to form in my mind of one of the most peculiar scenes imaginable: I could see my father carrying a Doberman pinscher to the back of a funeral car, where waiting for him were a vet, a nurse, and a mechanic. (I know, it sounds like the start of a joke, doesn't it?) A popping sound went off in my head and I was fully awake, but I couldn't get this vision out of my mind. I had no idea at the time that the mishmash of scenes I'd just seen was about to be explained by the day's events.

I'd just finished telling one of my co-workers at the salon about the strange dream, when in walked a man who told us that his dog had just been hit by a car. Fortunately, the dog was fine—and even luckier, the man driving the car was a vet who had immediately taken the dog to his office for a checkup. Yes, the dog was a Doberman pinscher. The man also told us that his girlfriend had gone with them, and since she was dressed to go to work, she was wearing her nurse's uniform.

No sooner had this happened than I got a phone call from my father, who told me that his oldest sister had died. He wondered if I could come and get him because he'd crashed his car on the way to see the funeral director.

My colleague looked at me in total disbelief when she heard what had happened to my father and realized that everything I'd told her earlier had unfolded within a matter of hours, even though my dream had been muddled, a bit of a collage of the day's events.

I'm sure that these experiences have nothing to do with my mediumship—even though as a medium, I've been given information about future events in people's lives. When the episodes of "second sight" occur, there's never any feeling of the spirit world around me; instead, I'm just aware that I'm witnessing something that's outside time. I hear no voices and sense no one, for it's a completely visual experience, other than a sound that resembles breathing, which vibrates at a loud, steady, rhythmic pace.

Seers of Tomorrow

I suppose that all of us at one time or another would like to see into our future, particularly when we're stuck at a crossroads in life—provided, that is, that we could be assured of seeing a favorable outcome (just like the many people who read their horoscopes every day, connecting to the good parts and disregarding the negative). But how certain can we be of the future? Is everything in our life predestined, or do we have the free will to shape our own fate?

One thing is for certain: Seers, oracles, and prophets have been a part of the human race since we first walked this planet. Some have been heralded as saints, while others have been burned at the stake for heresy. My own experiences of second sight have been random, but it still fascinates me whenever I have a precognitive dream or vision that actually comes true. How does this happen? As with all things relating to the unknown, the best way to gain understanding is to examine the evidence.

DARK VISIONS

One of the best examples of seership in Scottish history is that of Kenneth Mackenzie, better known as "the Brahan Seer," who was renowned throughout the Highlands in the 17th century for his gift of second sight.

The Seer's most famous prediction—which he made just before he was put to death on the orders of the Countess of Seaforth for alleged witchcraft—

was that the long line of Seaforths would end in extinction and sorrow; that the last chief of the line would be deaf and dumb; and that, although the chief would have four sons, they'd all die before him. The Seaforth lands would then pass from the male line to "a white-hooded lassie from the East" who would kill her own sister. Mackenzie then described the signs by which it would be known that these events were about to take place: certain physical deformities that would become apparent in four prominent Scottish landowners, who would be contemporaries of the last of the Seaforths.

More than 100 years later, the signs started to appear: The deformities were recognized in the four landowners whom the Seer had named; then Lieutenant-General Lord Francis Humberston Mackenzie, Baron Seaforth of Kintail, former British Governor of Barbados, went deaf after an attack of scarlet fever; and with frightening accuracy, the events foretold in the grim prediction were fulfilled one by one. After the untimely death of the last of his four sons, Lord Seaforth never spoke again. He died deaf and dumb on January 11, 1815, and his estate passed to his oldest surviving daughter, who returned hooded (as she was in mourning) from the East Indies, where her recently deceased husband, Admiral Sir Samuel Hood, had been in command of British naval forces. The last tragic part of the prediction came true when this "white-hooded lassie" was driving a carriage that was involved in an accident in which her sister, Lady Caroline Mackenzie, was killed.

This is but one of many prophecies attributed to the Brahan Seer that, although inconceivable at the time, have come to pass with astonishing accuracy.

Destiny or Predestiny?

The tragic nature of this tale is typical of many predictions of the future. It also suggests that there's no way to change the future, that certain events may already be predestined. Unlike divination, where the reader is trying to tap in to the future using a device or instruments, the person gifted with second sight doesn't try to make deliberate predictions, but simply sees the future under certain circumstances. Once while I was in a trance state, someone asked my spirit guide if he could predict the future. My guide replied that doing so was a 50-50 guess based on the feeling the person making the prediction had at that particular moment. But he then went on to describe a scene in the questioner's near future. Shocked, the individual asked how he was able to see into his life in such a way. My guide explained that in the spirit world, they have a much wider vision of life than we do and a better understanding of probability. Within days, his prediction came true.

✿ ✿ ✿

I believe that the gift of second sight differs greatly from that of clairvoyance or mediumship. Tarot-card readers or crystal-ball gazers offer readings of an intuitive nature, which depend upon their ability to gain information about a person psychically; then, using their own intuition, they make predictions based on their feelings. Mediums, on the other hand, must establish contact with relatives in the spirit world, who in certain circumstances may offer information regarding forthcoming events. In my experience, such information only comes when the recipient of the spirit message needs reassurance about the future. Either way, this type of "clear seeing," or *clairvoyance,* deals with predictions surrounding a person with a need. I'd suggest that it's the need that instigates the very predictions they seek.

Seership of the kind demonstrated by the Brahan Seer reaches much further forward in time and offers no comfort or guidance (also, the Seer needed no personal contact with the people involved). This type of prediction is additionally illustrated by Nostradamus, who gave accurate descriptions of certain events that took place during the French Revolution—even though he lived more than 200 years before the event. So there may be a difference in the ways in which people can see into the future and how far they can see. However, if we accept that even one person has truly seen future events, then we're left to ponder the nature of time itself.

THE WINDOW OF TIME

When someone tells you about an event that will happen in your life that you can't even imagine, and then it comes true, all you can think is, *How did they know that?* Is there some gap that appears in time that people can see through? Some of the forecasts given to me in my life certainly make me think so:

— When I was a child, my parents encountered a woman who described my future life to them, saying that I'd become well known as a clairvoyant and would demonstrate my gift in many places around the world. This has already happened, although at the time, neither my parents nor I even understood what a clairvoyant did.

— Upon entering a Spiritualist church for the first time in my early 20s at the request of a good friend, I was singled out by the medium and told that in five years' time I'd stand in that very church and do what the medium was doing. It was indeed five years later, almost to the day, that I gave one of my first demonstrations of clairvoyance in public.

— When my good friend and fellow medium Albert Best told me that he had a vision that I'd work in Japan, but not in his lifetime, I took no notice of him. But one year after Albert passed to the spirit world, I gave a public demonstration of mediumship in Tokyo.

— My friend Dronma, who is a psychic artist, turned to me one evening, sketch pad in hand, and showed me a drawing of an English springer spaniel. "This dog is for you, Gordon," she said. "I saw him sitting at your door, so I drew him for you." Nine months later, a friend asked if I'd take in a dog that needed a home. I went to see this animal, only to find out that it was a springer spaniel. On his kennel papers was his date of birth: December 9, 1995 . . . the very day that Dronma had drawn him for me.

This sort of thing has happened to me many times—far more often than coincidence would suggest—not to mention the many times I've made predictions for others and later found that they came true. Looking back at all these experiences, I've tried to understand how it works.

The Force Is with You

The more I consider the number of random episodes of second sight that happen to people when they least expect it, the more I see that we live as people in time and space, but there must be a part of our consciousness that exists outside these constraints.

A story told by Sir Alec Guinness comes to mind. He'd just spent many hours on a plane to New York and was feeling exhausted and hungry. He and his agent had already tried many restaurants without finding a free table when they entered a small Italian bistro. Once again they were told that there were no tables available. Sir Alec was almost ready to give up and return to his hotel for some much-needed sleep, when James Dean got up and kindly asked them to share his table. Before they sat down, Dean asked if they'd step outside the restaurant for a second, as he had something he'd like them both to see.

Outside was a sports car, which the young actor excitedly told them he'd just bought. Strangely, instead of congratulating him, Sir Alec said, in a voice he could hardly recognize, "Please never get in it. If you get in that car, you will be found dead in it by this time next week." This happened at 10 P.M. on Friday, September 23, 1955. The following Friday at 4 A.M., James Dean was found dead in that very same, albeit smashed, car.

Alec Guinness claimed never to have done anything like this before in his life and to have no idea how or why it happened to him. Remember, this happened before he found the Force in the *Star Wars* movie! My feeling is that it had to do with his state of mind at the time, that his fatigue opened his mind to a line of time concerning James Dean and the car. Most episodes of precognition occur when the mind is drifting between sleep and waking.

TRUTHS AND MISCONCEPTIONS ABOUT SECOND SIGHT

Myth #1: Little old ladies who live in tents can see into your future.

Some can, but seers can also wear business suits and Cartier jewelry and drive BMWs.

Myth #2: Anyone calling themselves a clairvoyant can give an accurate description of your future at will.

This isn't the case—more often than not, the genuine phenomenon is a random occurrence.

Myth #3: Seers can see everything about you just by looking at you.

No, this isn't true . . . so the skeletons in your closet are quite safe!

Myth #4: Certain items such as crystal balls, runes, or tarot cards will predict future events.

These are merely props that the seer focuses on. The real predictions come from within his or her mind.

Myth #5: Second sight is always considered a gift.

To those who really possess it, it can be a curse, since some of what they see may not be pleasant.

Myth #6: Always consult a clairvoyant before you get married.

Honestly, if you have to ask a clairvoyant this, the answer is no!

SEEING DOWN UNDER

Is second sight a natural faculty that's latent in everyone and is brought to the forefront when conditions are suitable for it to operate? I ask this because of the number of accounts I've heard from people who don't consider themselves to be psychic, yet have seen events before they've taken place.

An example of this came from a customer in a hairdressing salon where I worked in the mid-'80s.

While having her hair set, Mrs. Grove began to relate the story of how earlier that week she'd had a very peculiar experience—and it was the kind of tale that forced everyone to listen.

Mrs. Grove started out by saying that she'd been thinking of her daughter, who was studying at a university in the north of Scotland, when she'd fallen asleep in her chair. She found herself standing on top of the Sydney Opera House in Australia looking down at the harbor, where she could see her daughter and a young man sitting having a drink and laughing. The moment she began to question her dream, it ended, and she became fully awake again. By now all the salon's staff were tuned in to the tale and were waiting to hear what was so strange about it.

Our customer shared the second part of the story with us as she went to sit under the dryer. Two days after her dream, her daughter phoned to tell her that she was taking the next year off and was going with a friend to Australia for a break. Mrs. Grove said that she'd never experienced anything like this before in her life, and she had no explanation for how it could have happened.

Now, this may not be the most outstanding premonition the world has ever seen, but to our customer it was really amazing. As with most episodes of second sight, the seer was looking into a time that she didn't understand, because it was out of sync with her life. In this case, her daughter had already made her decision, so her future had been shaped, and plans had been put into action, but her mother was unaware of it. It's this type of experience that leads me to believe that those who see events before they happen actually experience them in a state of consciousness that's out of normal time.

I also feel that prophets and seers receive their visions when their minds are affected by certain emotional states, either their own or those of people around them. We only have to look at the Brahan Seer's last prophecy to have some indication of this, for he was about to be burned at the stake at the time. Imagine his feelings toward the family who had deemed him a witch and were now putting him to death: Was it because of the power of his emotions that he could see so far into the future and foretell the downfall of the family?

For the likes of Mrs. Grove, there wasn't the same emotional intensity, yet the feeling was still there. Her concern for her daughter's future led her mind to drift to a place in her child's life where she foresaw happiness for her.

I believe that most cases of second sight are born out of human emotion—from prophets such as Nostradamus to fortune-tellers with their cards and crystals—especially since most people who seek advice about the future do so because they're in the middle of some kind of dilemma or another.

Karmic Probability

An explanation that sits well with me is that predictions come from what I call "karmic probability." This is when we've made a decision or carried out an action that will steer us toward a particular point in life.

It's also my belief that most of our lives are in fact mapped out for us, but they're made up of many paths that reach out before us like strands of thread running through time—this allows us a certain amount of free will in our lives. Where some of these strands may connect to our own future, others will reach further in time, affecting events long after we're gone. The free will that people exercise in their lives is seen when the strands of time cross to form a junction, leaving the individuals to choose which threads to follow—much like standing in a train station and deciding how best to carry on a journey. People who have seen visions of the future have tapped in to certain strands of time and have seen particular junctions in a person's future—or even the future of generations to come.

I believe that everyone has this faculty. Even though it may be latent most of the time, it can come into play if the conditions are right. The feeling of knowing that something is about to happen—which I'm sure most people have experienced at some point in their life—is the first indicator, but the majority of people dismiss such thoughts or put them down to coincidence. If they'd only consider how many amazing accounts there are of second sight, and how many people have experienced it, both in the past and today, they might think differently about the subject.

Time is a long way from being fully understood, even though physics has come so far. Are there subtle dimensions within time itself? How much human consciousness is present? And how do certain people manage to see through time? The mechanics are little understood as yet, but what we *do* know is that such phenomena operate within certain boundaries and limitations. The seer can't see everything.

It's quite obvious to me that with our current knowledge of physics, we won't be able to even begin to approach this subject in the way we need to. However, having said that, at the rate that human consciousness is developing, I'd say that *it's only a matter of time.*

Chapter Nine

REINCARNATION

As I've mentioned, a fair amount of strange occurrences have happened in my life—many of which took place when I was young and had no real way of understanding what I was experiencing.

For example, the night before my 16th birthday I was spending time in London with my Aunt Sylvia and Uncle Mick. My uncle had been trying to surprise me by booking a day trip to Paris as a birthday present, but was finding it difficult to get tickets at such short notice. But even as I got ready for bed the night before, no one had breathed a word to me about the surprise.

In the early hours of the morning, I got up to go to the bathroom, and when I returned to bed I had the most vivid dream. I seemed to be falling, although it wasn't like such dreams I usually had, in which I'd hurtle fast toward the ground and wake up just before I crashed to the earth. In this case, I was falling backward, tumbling gently around and around. Then I was suddenly upright and moving forward in a sort of light until I passed right through a wall and found myself in a bar. The patrons looked as if they were in a movie set in World War II, for the men were in military uniforms and the women sported knee-length skirts. Some of the ladies wore scarves on their heads, while others had their hair rolled up at the back and waved on top, in the typical style of the '40s.

They appeared to be just babbling until, as if by magic, there was an adjustment to the sound. I could then hear some people speaking French, while others spoke English (some with American accents). At first I seemed to be walking around undetected, but then I noticed that someone was holding my hand and leading me through the crowded bar toward the far end, where some stairs led up to another level. I remember thinking, *Where am I?* as I heard a voice in the bar say, "Dieppe." I was none the wiser, as I'd never heard of Dieppe in my life.

The dream ended in an abrupt manner when the hand that seemed to be leading me pulled me so that I turned around and was looking in a mirror at two people holding hands—a young man in an Air

Force uniform, and a blonde girl of about the same age. They were looking back at me in the mirror when they abruptly both magnified in size and advanced toward me, until I felt the woman walk right through me. This made my head burst with an almighty sound that shot me out of the dream, and I found myself sitting up in bed.

I didn't mention the dream to my aunt or uncle in the morning—in fact, I forgot all about it as soon as my aunt came in and wished me happy birthday and told me that I must get up soon because there was a surprise for me. I was told that I was being taken to France for the day by my uncle, but we'd have to leave very soon to drive to the coast and catch the ferry. It turned out that my uncle had been unable to book the trip to Paris, so instead he'd decided to take me to Boulogne.

I remember being so excited . . . until, that is, we reached the dock and were told that we'd missed the morning trip and would have to wait until the afternoon for the next one. My uncle was very disappointed and was about to come up with some new idea for a birthday treat when a man at the dock came over and told him that if we could drive down the coast to Newhaven, we might still catch the boat across to Dieppe.

When I heard the word *Dieppe,* something inside me exploded, and my heart almost stopped. My uncle asked me if I was all right, but I said nothing as we ran to the car and sped off along the coast at high speed. Somehow we managed to reach the boat on time, so we quickly settled down for the crossing. I'd never been out of the UK in my life—I couldn't wait to get to France so that when I got back to Scotland I could tell my brothers I'd been to a foreign land.

Arriving at the port in Dieppe turned out to be the oddest experience because my uncle said that we should find somewhere nice to have lunch, and I replied, "Well, we're going in the wrong direction—the best cafés are up to the right."

Uncle Mick looked at me in a very strange way indeed, but followed my lead. I really did know the place somehow, and soon I'd led us to a very chic café . . . which turned out to be exactly the same as the one in the dream I'd had hours earlier. When I noticed the stairs leading to the upper level, I told my uncle that I had to go upstairs and look in the large mirror. It wasn't visible from where we were standing, but when I got to the top of the stairs, there it was.

Sitting in that café made me feel so overwhelmingly sad because I kept remembering places and events that somehow belonged to me, yet how could they? Faces would flash in my mind, along with names and the sound of voices. Just as in the dream, different languages and accents were all running around in my head, and I felt happy and sad in turn, as if a life were passing before me. My uncle asked why I'd gotten so quiet, and it dawned on me that this was my birthday! I was supposed to be happy, so I had to clear my mind of this stuff.

We left the café soon after and were shopping for gifts for my mother and aunt, when again, Uncle Mick suggested a certain route, and I told him no, as there was only a church down that road. Again he gave me an odd look. We walked around the corner, and there was the old church, just as I'd said. This sort of thing happened for the rest of the day, and I had no idea why I remembered so much about a place I'd never been to before. Even at that age, I'd already experienced episodes of mediumship and had picked up psychic messages for other people, but this was very different. It was just like remembering something from my own past.

I felt exhausted when we got back on the boat, and I slept all the way back to England and then again in the car to London and right on through the night. The following morning I woke up feeling wonderful, refreshed, and somehow lighter.

I think of what happened in Dieppe whenever I'm asked about reincarnation. To this day this is the only experience I've had that may or may not have been some kind of past-life memory. I'm still not sure, but having looked at the subject now for many years—hopefully with an open mind—it seems to me that there are too many supporting cases coming to light for past-life memories to all be coincidence.

LIVING WITH THE PAST

The idea of reincarnation has been around for thousands of years. It was an accepted part of Christianity until the sixth century, when the Byzantine emperor Justinian threw the weight of his support behind an opposing doctrine—after that, anyone found preaching reincarnation would be excommunicated. It wasn't until the 13th century that the idea appeared again among the Christian sect known as the Cathars. The Catholic Church subsequently directed a crusade against them, killing hundreds of thousands of people of the Languedoc region of France. Is it any wonder that the Catholic soldiers were reluctant to accept reincarnation, which according to Eastern religions works on the basis of taking responsibility for your own actions?

The idea has, however, been examined more carefully in recent times. Perhaps one of the best known of the current researchers into the subject is Dr. Ian Stevenson. To date, he's investigated several thousand cases of children who have spontaneously recalled previous lives. Dr. Stevenson's methodology is sound, and he's developed many techniques that enable him to determine if the child could have learned the so-called memories through ordinary means, and to check out the details of the past life.

Some of the children have been able to pinpoint exact streets and houses from their past lives, even though they were in places that these kids had never been to in this life. Some have also been able to talk to people from their past lives in a way unique to the dead person they were claiming to be. In addition, Dr. Stevenson found that many of the children who remembered a past life would be born in this life with a scar or birthmark relating to suffering in the former.

HEALING OLD SCARS

Carol Bowman's book *Children's Past Lives* also gives many accounts of children who remembered former lives. Carol's first encounter with this happened when her five-year-old son, Chase, suddenly developed an inexplicable fear of fireworks. Sometime later that year, a hypnotherapist happened to be visiting her, so Carol told him about it. He had experience in past-life hypnotic regression with adults, so he asked if he could try something similar with the boy.

With no need for hypnotic induction, Carol's son responded to questions put to him by the therapist: He recalled being a soldier carrying a gun, which he described as having a sword on the end of it. Then he described a pain in his wrist (which in this life had been affected by eczema ever since he was a baby). In the past life, he remembered flashing lights of gunfire around him and being shot in the wrist. Within a few days of the recall experience, his eczema completely disappeared, as did his fear of fireworks.

※ ※ ※

Adults can also be helped by past-life therapy. In his book *Many Lives, Many Masters,* Dr. Brian Weiss relates the case of Catherine, a young patient of his who had been suffering from nightmares and chronic anxiety attacks. After treating her with all the traditional forms of medicine, Dr. Weiss turned to hypnosis. During the sessions, he was astonished as Catherine began to relive the past-life traumas that seemed to hold the key to her present problems.

While in a hypnotic trance, Catherine was able to give accurate descriptions of her previous lives, along with the traumas she'd suffered in them, which had linked to her fears in this life. This was amazing enough, but in certain sessions she'd also arrive at a between-life stage and channel information from spirits of a much higher consciousness, who would give Dr. Weiss more information about his patient and even mention details about the doctor's own life, which no one else was aware of.

Most fascinating was the effect that past-life memories were having on Catherine. One of her greatest phobias was of water—specifically, choking on it—to the extent that she couldn't take pills for fear of choking to death. During one session, she remembered a life from 1800 B.C., where she'd been drowning and had eventually choked to death. After this session, her fear lessened considerably, and in no time, she was cured of her phobia altogether.

In a short period of time, Catherine underwent many hypnotic sessions in which she remembered many different lives and the difficulties she'd endured in them—and each episode allowed her to cast off more of her present anxiety. In one session, Dr. Weiss asked his patient if she could tell him how many times she'd lived on Earth. She replied, "Eighty-six." The doctor then asked why she'd only tapped in to 12 of those, and was told by the entranced Catherine that these were the only ones that needed to be concluded—the other 70 or so had no bearing on where she was now.

If all this is seen as evidence that we've lived before, then we must think that we'll live again. And as long as serious men and women of science continue their studies into past-life recall, then at some point we may find a way of knowing more about who we once were and how that's affecting who we are now.

BLASTS FROM THE PAST

The sad thing about this subject is that it's often abused by the deluded "psychic vultures" who prey on people who have emotional needs. For example, at a seminar in Germany around 1997, I encountered a woman who was giving talks and personal sessions of past-life regression. At first I thought nothing of it, but about halfway through the week, I overheard one of the people who was attending the course comment that she'd been told by the past-life woman that she was Mary, Queen of Scots in her previous life. I smiled to myself and thought, *Not another one of those.* (It always seems to be famous people who come up in past-life stuff—a bit like mediums who insist on having spirit guides such as Jesus, St. Peter, or Confucius. Why not Joe Smith who was a street cleaner in 1900 or something?)

As we came to the end of the week, it turned out that masses of people attending the seminar had gone for past-life sessions with the woman—at about $100 a pop—and everyone I encountered had been told about their famous past life as Joan of Arc, Henry VIII, or any number of kings and queens from European history. Oh, the odd woman was told of a life of prostitution, but I'm sure that this past-life "expert" only did this to spite the prettier women at the seminar. It was unbelievable that so many people bought into this scam, so I had to go and see the woman for myself.

She began by telling me that I was psychic (not bad . . . especially considering that she'd watched me give a demonstration of mediumship earlier in the week). Then she asked if I had any health problems. I told her that my left eye sometimes got infected, and she told me that she was seeing me on a ship at the Battle of Trafalgar—I was Admiral Nelson!

"Didn't he lose his *right* eye?" I asked.

She looked very upset that I dared question her and told me to be quiet and wait, as the visions were changing. After about a half minute of saying, "Ah yes, ah yes," to herself, she told me that I'd been a prostitute—and not a very high-class one at that. I asked her where she was getting her information, and she replied, "The Masters." I assumed that was the name of the bank or association where she invested all her money!

Truths and Misconceptions about Reincarnation

Myth #1: Dreams of people and places from the past mean that you're revisiting a past life.
Not necessarily—chances are that you've acquired these visions from a book, conversation, or movie. Think about it!

Myth #2: Everybody was someone famous in their past lives.

Darling, we can't all have been Cleopatra!

Myth #3: Exotic past lives make you more interesting.

If you can really remember a past life, then you're probably repeating mistakes from that life, and the memory is a warning to tie up the loose ends and get on with *this* life.

Myth #4: Who you were in a past life is more important than who you are now.

All you are now is an accumulation of all you've been.

Myth #5: If you're bad in this life, you may come back as an animal.

Actually, some animals are more enlightened than humans are.

Myth #6: Being successful in this life guarantees success in the next.

No, in a future life you may have to face more difficult times in order for your consciousness to expand.

NATIONS REMEMBER

To understand past-life memories and the effects they may be having on the here-and-now, you must first accept the existence of consciousness. As the Dalai Lama, the spiritual leader of Tibet, says in his book *The Way to Freedom:*

> If we come to understand that the continuity of the consciousness cannot be exhausted in one lifetime, we will find that there is logical support for the possibility of life after death. If we are not convinced of the continuity of consciousness, at least we know that there is no evidence that can disprove the theory of life after death. We cannot prove it, but we cannot disprove it. There are many cases of people remembering their past lives vividly. It is not a phenomenon confined to Buddhists. There are people with such memories whose parents do not believe in life after death or past lives. I know of three cases of children who have been able to remember their past lives vividly. In one case the recollection of the past life was so vivid that even though the parents previously did not believe in life after death, as a result of the clarity of their child's recollections, they are now convinced.

I do believe that many of us are influenced by past emotional experiences, whether we remember them or not, which still have an impact on the present. I've come to learn that places also hold memories of past events: I'm certain that traumatic events such as wars and massacres leave a stain in the consciousness of a place (or even a country or continent) that can be picked up by the people living there. Just as ghosts are emotional stains that have been left imprinted on time and space, so too can a nation have emotional stains imprinted on the consciousness of that place.

A Spirit World or a World of Spirit?

Back in 1997 I was working as a tutor at the Arthur Findlay College for Psychic Studies, when I noticed that there was to be a lecture on reincarnation given by two men—one was the editor of *Reincarnation* magazine, and the other was from the College of Psychic Studies in London. As the subject always raises great debate among Spiritualists, I thought it would be interesting to go along and listen.

In the rather grand library room, about 80 people were crammed into every available seat to listen to the lecture. The man from the college spoke clearly about consciousness and energy and used a scientific approach, whereas the editor talked more about the religious side of reincarnation and the law of cause and effect. The intensity in the room was growing, as I could feel the people in the crowd anxiously waiting to ask questions. When the time came to do so, almost every hand rose in the air at once. The first question—which was to be expected—

was: "If we reincarnate, then who are mediums contacting in the spirit world?"

The man from the College for Psychic Studies explained that consciousness has many layers, and the physical form is only a small part of the overall energy field of an individual consciousness. At death, a person's spirit returns to its overall higher consciousness with memories of its recent life, yet the higher consciousness can also project spirit energy into a new physical life at the same time.

If this is true, then it would have to mean that one consciousness could give life to many people at the same time. This can be linked to the idea of a soul group, where many people are working from the same higher consciousness at the same time, and each one has come into the material world with the same goal or purpose.

Many other questions were asked that day, such as what time span was involved between each rebirth, why did we need to live so many lives in the physical world, and who decided if we should reincarnate? The answers that were given pleased some people but not all. Nevertheless, at the end of the lecture, we were asked to put up our hands if we believed in reincarnation—and I was quite surprised to see that at least 90 percent of the people in that room raised their hands. About the same number again admitted to feeling that this wasn't their first life on Earth.

Right after that lecture, I began to think about consciousness being more universal than each individual person . . . and I wondered what was really beyond death. I knew that I'd seen, heard, and sensed spirits all my life, and I'd been given messages from spirits that were very accurate and had helped many people through their bereavement, but was that all there was to the human spirit? And what about the spirit world: Was it just an in-between stage where spirits adjusted before moving on to the next level? Or could it be that we're living in a world of spirit right now in our human form and we don't even recognize it, so we have to come tumbling back for life after life until we can understand it all?

When I left the Arthur Findlay College at the end of the week, I knew that I had to look more deeply into the subject.

※ ※ ※

Since that day in 1997, I've studied the religions that believe in reincarnation and the scientific studies on the subject, and I've also listened to many people's accounts of past-life recall. The one thing that comes to my mind whenever I think of people who remember a previous life is *Why?* Why are memories, which are almost always traumatic, still haunting the mind in its new incarnation?

I believe it can only be that there's unfinished business to be settled. I know that it's the people who die unexpectedly and have things left to wrap up in this life who communicate best through a medium. Their intention is always to tie up all their loose ends so that they can move on spiritually. It may be that the past-life episodes that are remembered are those that need to be healed in order to allow progression of the human spirit—which would explain the findings of people such as Dr. Brian Weiss.

If we've lived many lives in many countries and different cultures, it may also be that when we revisit these places, some memory is triggered. This may have been what happened to me in Dieppe— only the visions appeared prior to my being told I was gong there (unless such episodes can be perceived by the unconscious mind ahead of time?).

I go back to what the Dalai Lama says: "To understand the nature of rebirth, you first have to understand consciousness." I look at consciousness as being like the hard drive of a computer: It has masses of memory, so even when one program is being run on the screen, there are still many available on the hard drive—some of which have been run before, and some of which will be run in the future. By looking at consciousness in this way, I can see that as a medium, even when I'm using one program, I can still access files from other programs. So the memories of a person who has died can be accessed from their consciousness databases and relayed back to their loved ones, even if they've now reincarnated into another body. In this sense, mediumship is the ability to tap in to the spiritual hard drive.

When I look at things in this way, I have no problem understanding that we have a greater consciousness (the main computer if you like), which houses all that we've ever done in all our lives. Past-life memory might then interfere with our current program, or life, which would have to be put right in order for our current program to run smoothly.

The thing about reincarnation is that it's a system of refining life actions and learning from mistakes. It encourages those who believe in it to take responsibility for all their actions so as to create good karma and allow their consciousness to expand and grow. Otherwise, we'll only repeat the same lessons until we've finally learned them.

What makes this idea sometimes difficult to accept is our natural human emotions: They often blind us to the bigger picture and close our minds so that we think all we are is someone who may or may not have lived before, and who may or may not live again.

Because of what I've experienced in my life as a medium, I know that I'm more than this. I know that even though my physical body will die one day, *I* will not. I know that my spirit will learn from all that I've experienced in this life as Gordon Smith and will add that program to the memory in my spiritual database. My next program might run in a more subtle spirit world of light, or it may run back here on Earth. I don't have the words to describe the stages I'll go through after death, but one thing I can say is that I'm conscious of living *now,* and that's what's most important.

※ ※

Chapter Ten

CONSCIOUSNESS

rying to understand ourselves isn't easy—after all, we must be one of the greatest mysteries there's ever been. Are we humans who will live in a spirit world after we die, or are we spirits who are currently living a human life?

Questions such as these and many more were running through my head while I was driving to the countryside back in 1992, during a period in my life when I felt cut off from everything and everyone. It was one of those times when nothing seemed to make sense, the kind of experience that most of us go through when we feel that the world's closing in on us and we just need a reality check.

I was driving my car that day without really concentrating on where I was going, and my mind was clouded with thoughts of *What's it all about?* and *There's got to be more to life than this.* Let's face it, I was having a bad hair day! I pulled my car off the side of the road in the Campsie Glen, a quiet place not more than a half hour's drive to the north of Glasgow. I often went there to escape from the world: Its beautiful hills, glens, and waterfalls cascading through rugged ravines were always a welcoming sight. The hills weren't alive with the sound of music that day—in fact, they were devoid of people, which was just what I wanted. I had to get away from the city, all the people in my life, and all the thoughts that were clouding my brain.

I felt as though I had every worry of the world on my shoulders: the end of my marriage, thoughts of my children, and uncertainty about what I was doing in my life as a medium. I just didn't feel that I had any foundation, and more than that, I didn't have a clue as to what was real and what wasn't. I sat alone next to a large waterfall with my head slumped, and I asked out loud, "What am I all about?"

I remember taking a deep breath and trying to meditate, but all I wanted to do was cry. So many problems rushed through my mind at once, and again I thought, *What am I all about?* Then I just sat for a while listening to the roar of the waterfall, the sound rushing through me until I felt that it had almost become part of my thinking.

All of a sudden I became aware of the sound of a branch creaking in the distance and a tiny trickle of water some ten feet from where I was sitting. It was as if someone had turned the waterfall off, yet they hadn't. Without lifting my head, I could tell which tree the creaking sound was coming from, and not only was I aware of the trickling stream, but I could describe every stone the water was rippling over. I was seeing every blade of grass around me individually, yet I wasn't actually looking at any of them. A sense of calm ran through me like nothing I'd ever felt before. Suddenly I was alive—awake to the life around me and the life within me. I felt connected to everything: Every living thing was a part of me, and I was a part of it.

This was one of the most amazing feelings I'd ever experienced, greater than seeing spirits or watching inanimate objects fly around a room. I was conscious of life, not phenomena. I *felt* alive, as if this was the real me—a me that had always existed but had never been able to come to the surface. All the times I'd tried to meditate and thought that I'd achieved a state of spiritual ecstasy simply paled in comparison. My mind had expanded until I seemed to be way beyond my physical body—but I wasn't having an out-of-body experience, nor was I in a state of trance that I could associate with discarnate spirits. This was the real deal: My spirit was in touch with all the life around me. This was the first time

I'd felt what it was like to be consciously aware. It was mind-blowing.

I left the glen on the most amazing high. All at once I'd gained an understanding of myself that I'd never had before, even though I'd seen and sensed things that other people couldn't. But now I was aware of myself as a spirit in the material world.

From that moment on, I felt compelled to investigate my own spirit in the same way that I'd looked into life after death in order to help others. I needed to know the truth, for I knew that it would help people understand more about the nature of life and death, and about consciousness itself.

Fear and Limitation

For years I'd witnessed visions and heard spirit voices, and based on the evidence I'd given people through my mediumship, I knew there was a life after physical death. But the overwhelming feeling I'd just experienced at Campsie Glen gave me a much wider view of the human spirit. It made my belief more concrete, but more than that, I began to look at life in a completely different way. I could see how in spirit form we have a greater connection to all of life and have a much broader vision, which is why spirits on the Other Side can give us information about future events and answers to problems that might seem insurmountable to us. I could understand how consciousness is capable of producing phenomena that the human mind can't explain. And I could see how a mind that has experienced even a moment of expansion becomes more accepting of the so-called supernatural.

My experience was just a glimpse, I'm sure, of what our minds are capable of when they're not restricted by our emotions. The concerns and worries we experience in this life become the limiting force that stops us from accepting what we're capable of at our best. Fear keeps the human mind earthbound, yet there's so much for us to tap in to and grow toward if we can only allow ourselves to become less limited in our thinking.

Many people today tend to live inside their heads. Their entire world is governed by their thoughts, many of which end up becoming fears and anxieties: worries about not having enough material goods or concerns about others' judgments. This type of thinking keeps the mind running around and around like a wheel—never expanding, but only repeating patterns of limited, fearful thoughts, which the mind then becomes accustomed to and can't release.

Something a Buddhist monk once told me is a prime example of how some people can never let go of their concerns. The monk was repeating a story he'd overheard about two monks who'd taken a vow of celibacy. This vow forbade them to have any contact with women, to the point that they weren't even allowed to shake hands. One morning the two monks were returning to the monastery when they came across a young woman who was stuck halfway across a stream. She looked toward the monks for help, but knowing the religious order they came from, she realized that she couldn't ask them for assistance. Yet one of the monks moved quickly in her direction, lifted her in his arms, and carried her to the other side.

After the evening prayers back at the monastery, the two monks were sitting together when one turned to the other and said, "I can't get it out of my head that you carried that young woman across the river this morning."

The other replied, "I left her there this morning. You're still carrying her, it would seem."

Learning to let go of your concerns is the first step in allowing your consciousness to expand. Letting go of situations you can't change will also gently open up your mind to other levels of consciousness.

TRUTHS AND MISCONCEPTIONS ABOUT CONSCIOUSNESS

Myth #1: The human brain is our consciousness.

Not so—*all* we are is consciousness. The brain is just a tiny part of that.

Myth #2: Consciousness is only a part of our lives.

The reality is that our *lives* are only a part of consciousness.

Myth #3: Consciousness is limited by time and space.

Consciousness is vast and many-layered. Our waking human consciousness, if measured in the scale of things, would be like a tiny grain of sand.

Myth #4: Consciousness is fixed and unchanging.

Consciousness is ever-changing, ever-growing—it's we who seem to be static by comparison.

Myth #5: Only humans are conscious.

Consciousness is the life force that runs through the universe. All life is a part of it. To cause harm to anything within it must surely cause harm to ourselves.

Myth #6: There's no need to explore our own consciousness.

Every living being is driven to expand its own consciousness as part of the greater whole.

The Mind Doctor

The famous psychologist Carl Gustav Jung spent many years journeying through his own consciousness. From childhood on, the Swiss scientist was aware of being two different personalities: one who lived in the outer world, went to school, and was more or less the same as many other boys; and one who was more grown-up, skeptical, and withdrawn from the physical world. Somehow he felt that his second persona, which he described as his *inner personality,* was more in touch with the beauty of nature and connected to the vast undiscovered universe and everything that lived within it.

After many years of investigation, Jung discovered that this inner subconscious mind was connected to a higher mind, which he called *the collective unconscious.* He described this as a store of knowledge of everything past, present, and future (or "the hard drive" I was talking about earlier). Jung felt that the collective unconscious was the reason people became aware of similar information at the same time, even if they were living in different parts of the globe. Like the subconscious mind, the collective unconscious could communicate with the individual mind through dreams and other symbolic ways.

First Emotion

A big part of my spiritual journey has been an investigation into my inner self, looking at the emotional part of my life in order to find out more about the workings of my own mind. Much like Jung, I can remember two different personalities when I was a kid: one that behaved in a childlike way; and a much more mature, thoughtful self that seemed to take note of things happening around me and that recorded each situation before filing it away. I've found that it's this part of my mind that's connected to the psychic side of my nature.

When I first began to learn about mediumship, I learned that it was important to empty my mind so that it could be used as a clear screen for the spirit world to project images on. Our conscious mind is often clouded by our traumatic emotional memories—which we must learn to release, since they can fester and restrict the consciousness. For a medium, they'll also interfere with messages coming in from the spirit world. So I undertook the task of sorting through my mind to try to find out how many of my emotional memories were relevant to me in the here-and-now, and how much was just junk that was taking up space.

※ ※ ※

My first conscious memory goes back to when I was four years old. My mother and I were returning from the local shops around midmorning, and we'd just started walking up the path leading to the front door of our home, when I remember a feeling of fear ran through me.

By the time my mother and I had reached the door, this feeling of foreboding overwhelmed me. Looking back, I'm sure it came from something I sensed in my mother's behavior. She felt that someone was in the house and hesitated for a moment before entering. I clearly remember that she told me to stand still as she opened the door wide and called out that she knew someone was there. Standing in the open doorway, she called out again, saying that she was sending for the police. I can still remember standing there wondering what was going on—feeling, I suppose, more afraid for my mother than for myself.

It could only have been seconds later that we heard noises coming from one of the bedrooms in the house. A neighbor heard the commotion and came sprinting down the path to join us, just as we caught sight of a young man running off through our back garden and disappearing down the lane. It appeared that my mother had disturbed him before he could do much, because when she and the neighbor searched the house, they found that nothing had been taken or damaged. The only sign that the man had been there was the open window in the bedroom, which he'd used to enter and leave our home.

It's quite strange to look back and find that this was truly the first time I was aware of having a feeling. To me, this first emotion is an awakening of the mind—it's the consciousness fusing with the physical world, bringing the person straight into the reality of this life. The mind of every young child, I feel, drifts in and out of different states of consciousness before it connects fully with this physical life. This is why it's often difficult to recall our early lives in any detail.

EMOTIONAL GARBAGE

One of the most important things I learned when I began to develop my abilities as a medium was meditation, which taught me a great deal about myself. When I first began the practice, even though I found it easy to sit still and breathe well, it still took me some time to come to terms with quieting the thoughts in my head. This was the most difficult part of the discipline for me to master: The more I'd try to empty my mind of thoughts, the more I'd find my head filled with sounds and visions. Instead of a still, peaceful visualization of calm and serenity, my head would feel like the first day of the January sales in London—with memories, dreams, and reflections all scrambling to get to the forefront of my conscious mind.

As I continued to meditate, I found that I would just fall asleep. This was due to the mental exhaustion I experienced trying to keep thoughts out of my head. I soon learned that the mind has muscles just like the body, so if you overexercise muscles that haven't been used much before, then you're bound to feel the effects of overexertion. And, along with falling asleep, I'd often complain of headaches at the start—again, my aching mind muscles were reminding me to pace myself.

After about six months of practicing meditation, I began to relax and allow my mind to ease into it. I no longer felt in such a hurry to learn because I'd calmed down, and I noticed that fewer thoughts were cramming into my head. Even better, I'd learned to let them pass through like clouds blowing in the wind. These thoughts and images were only my emotional garbage. I was learning to let it all go, whereas before I would have held on to it all, as most people do. But it's only when we can let go of all our stored mind rubbish that we can begin to catch a glimpse of our true selves. I often think of this when I'm clearing out a cupboard in my home and I find things I haven't used for years and probably will never use again.

Just like cleaning one's home, emptying the mind of its clutter creates a feeling of lightness and space. It's the first step toward understanding consciousness. For instance, after about a year of clearing out my emotional mind garbage, I began to notice many changes in my behavior, both in how I viewed myself and how I treated others. I found myself becoming more patient and less likely to react to emotional scenes. Whereas once I would have become involved in everybody's dramas without thinking, now I seemed to be more conscious of the underlying reasons for others' emotional outbursts, so I'd be detached and calm in my own responses. I also began to find that I was much less sentimental than I'd ever been before. By clearing my mind of old mental garbage, I became much more balanced. I realized that the emotional detachment I was now aware of was something I had to develop further if I were to work as a medium, as I'd be no good to anyone if I became immersed in other people's grief.

Guiding Light

Emptying your mind of its old conditioning is a preparation for reaching its higher, more subtle states. It was when I'd done this that I began to go into a trance and became more aware of the spirit guides, teachers, and higher energies around me. I often wondered if they were actually a part of my own higher mind, or were separate entities who were able to link with me because I'd become more open-minded, so to speak. It may be a moot point, because at some level of consciousness we're all one anyway. This became clearer to me when I listened to a tape of a trance session given by one of my spirit guides back in 2001.

During this particular session, I'd gone into a trance for a group of people at the Spiritualist Association of Great Britain, and my main guide, Chi, had come through to talk to the assemblage. One man asked him to explain the nature of consciousness. Chi's explanation was as follows:

> Consciousness is what you are right now. This very moment is as conscious as you are of yourself. The mind in the human state of consciousness is limited and does not like to go beyond what it knows as reality. Anything beyond your understanding of reality can cause you disturbance because your mind wants to dissect any phenomenon and understand it through reason and rationality, but reason and rationality will limit you from understanding the experience itself.
>
> You must remember that consciousness is life, and as such, is many-leveled. To gain more understanding of such a vast thing, you must know where you are in it yourself. As a human being, you are aware of many things that are less conscious and less aware than you are in your world, but cannot fathom that there are other forms of consciousness that are more conscious of themselves and even more aware of where they exist within reality. Even

in this moment, as I speak with you through the body of this medium, are you conscious of me as a separate spirit entity, or as a higher part of the mind of the medium—or neither? What does your own conscious mind accept of this experience?

The fact is, I am both separate and connected to the mind of the medium, as are you in this moment; the fact that you cannot see me as a person, spirit, or in human form does not mean that I do not exist. And if I were to appear to you in this room this very moment, it would not convince you of my existence either if you were not ready to integrate such a happening into your consciousness.

The nature of consciousness is what you should ponder, as it is expanding just like the universe in all directions without fear of limitation. To know more of yourself in any given moment, you must become like nature itself, ever-growing and renewing. Life and death are but segments of the entire process.

Chi also talked of the mind in human form being like a small transistor radio, while the bigger consciousness that feeds it was like a massive power station that couldn't connect fully to the small receiver, since so much power would blow it completely. He also mentioned that spiritual teachers such as Christ and the Buddha were like adapters who filtered down some of the power and inspired us to try to understand more of the conscious mind.

CRYSTAL CLEAR

My vision of consciousness has certainly changed over the years. I remember that when I first started out as a medium, I thought that the spirits who communicated through me lived in a very well-lit Victorian spirit world, that they still resembled people, and that they'd be waiting there for everyone they loved to cross over. Many years and many communications later, I have a much broader idea of consciousness during this life and the one beyond.

I think it all began to change for me when I had one of my funny dreams in 1993 (I call them that because when they're occurring, they mean absolutely nothing to me, but much later they prove to be very significant). Looking now at the dream journal I keep next to my bed, I see that very dream noted in detail. I'd titled it "The Diamond," and at the top of the page I'd made a note: "Asking about consciousness." (Something I try to do if I remember a very vivid dream is to note what was prominent in my mind prior to having it—this time it had been the subject of consciousness.)

My dream began with my death: I witnessed myself leaving my body, which lay motionless on a bed. I had no awareness of any spirit body or vehicle, just consciousness. In this state I moved into a light where I could just make out the silhouettes of people who appeared to be made of the same light.

This resembled my own idea of the spirit world.

I was lifted high above this world of light, and I began to notice what looked like crystals. There were millions of these perfectly clear-cut stones, all individual and yet all connected by strands of light. These strands, I noticed, were also reaching down into the world of light people below, as if connecting them to the masses of crystals. Somehow I'd become connected, too: I was part of one of the multifaceted stones. It felt as if my "self" was one of the many facets, yet I knew that I was all of the crystal at one and the same time. (Well, I said it was a funny dream!)

A beam of light passed through my crystal, and suddenly it was a collage of holograms and images of people from different times. Some I could recognize by their outfits, while others I couldn't place— but all the time I was experiencing a certain knowing, as if these were my memories.

The dream changed at this point, and I was separated from the crystal and moving at very high speed toward something in the distance below me. It was a woman who was working as a medium, only she was inside a crystal, and there were lots of people in crystals trying to link to one of the facets that encompassed her. All the people in crystals, including me, had a strand of golden light connecting them to each other, and this also connected us to where I had just come from.

I never got to link with the mind of the medium in my dream. Instead, I was pulled back to my body at such a rate that I woke with a start, and found that I was sitting up in my bed in a cold sweat, heart pounding.

THE DIAMOND

Not long after my crystal dream I was visiting Dronma, my psychic-artist friend who is also a Tibetan Buddhist. When I told her of my experience of being connected to people inside crystals, she produced a series of drawings she'd done over the years, some of which showed people inside crystals all connected to one another, and others showing the universe as interconnecting crystals. I could hardly believe it! She also told me that this had helped her understand the nature of consciousness.

I have no problem with the idea that all living things are connected, and that it's life that connects us, especially after my experience in the Campsie Glen. I also believe that our life force never dies and that Jung's collective unconscious stores everything that has ever occurred. My way of looking at this is that the memories of each life are kept on file, while the life force itself goes on, either in a spirit dimension or back here in the form of another physical life.

If our consciousness is like a diamond, then I feel that one of the purposes of this journey is to polish it—and we can do so by learning more about ourselves. I'm also sure that every bad deed in this life will take away some of the luster from the stone, but every good one will make it sparkle.

SO WHAT NOW?

When I look over all the amazing things that have happened in my life and in the lives of others, I realize that there's much more to us than meets the eye. So many people throughout history have experienced glimpses of what the human spirit is capable of producing by way of miracles and other phenomena that defy every physical law. I believe that so-called supernatural mysteries have been given to us so that we can learn more about our supernature, our spirituality, which is our destiny to encounter.

The more I realize that my life now is but one tiny program running from a vast source of spiritual consciousness, the less worried I am about experiencing everything I can in this lifetime, for I know that my soul will go on and on beyond the change we call "death." I'm not surprised when I hear of extraordinary events in this world or witness people who display exceptional spiritual gifts and abilities because I accept that consciousness is developing at different levels in different people—some will ripen sooner than others, but each individual will have his or her chance to grow when ready.

If we open our minds to all things, then we may experience the unbelievable . . . and find that it's the truth.

Acknowledgments

To Meg, for providing me with the inspiration for this book, to Jo for looking after me so well, to Michelle for her nurturing guidance, to Reid and Leon for their vision, and to all the other Hay House employees for their hard work and constant support.

To Ros, thank you for your support and, more important, your friendship.

To Dronma, for being you.

To Tricia and Archie, for your help and your wonderful stories.

To my son Paul, thank you for your help and your patience!

And a special thank you to Lizzie for all your hard work and perseverance.

Further Reading

Alighieri, Dante, *The Divine Comedy,* Oxford Paperbacks, 1998

Armour, Mary, *Helen Duncan: My Living Has Not Been in Vain,* Pembridge Publishing, 2001

Bowman, Carol, *Children's Past Lives,* Bantam Books, 1997

Brealey, Gena, with Kay Hunter, *Two Worlds of Helen Duncan,* Regency Press, 1985

Cheetham, Erika (trans. and ed.), *The Prophecies of Nostradamus,* Corgi, 1988

Flint, Leslie, *Voices in the Dark,* Two Worlds Publishing Co. Ltd., 2000

Hawking, Stephen, *A Brief History of Time,* Bantam Books, 1998

His Holiness the Dalai Lama, *The Way to Freedom,* Thorsons, 1997

Kennedy, David, *A Venture in Immortality,* Colin Smythe Ltd., 1973

Mackenzie, Alexander, *The Prophecies of the Brahan Seer,* Sutherland Press, 1972

Matt, Daniel C., *God & the Big Bang,* Jewish Lights Publishing, 1996

Moacanin, Radmila, *The Essence of Jung's Psychology and Tibetan Buddhism: Western and Eastern Paths to the Heart,* Wisdom Publications, 2003

Moody, Jr., M.D., Raymond A., *Life after Life,* Corgi, 1975

Pike, James, *The Other Side,* W. H. Allen, 1969

Rinpoche, Kalu, *Secret Buddhism: Vajrayana Practices,* ClearPoint Press, 1995

Roy, Archie, *A Sense of Something Strange,* Dog and Bone, 1990

——, *Archives of the Mind,* SNU Publications, 1996

Twigg, Ena, *The Woman Who Shocked the World*

Weiss, M.D., Brian, *Many Lives, Many Masters,* Piatkus Books, 1994

Wilson, Colin, *The Occult,* Watkins Publishing, 2003

About the Author

*G*ordon Smith, the author of *Spirit Messenger,* is an astoundingly accurate medium who's renowned for his ability to give exact names of people, places, and even streets. The seventh son of a seventh son, Gordon travels all around the world demonstrating his abilities, offering healing and comfort to thousands of people. At the end of his journeys, he returns to his native Glasgow where he runs a barbershop. As Gordon says, there's nothing like a short back and sides for keeping his feet firmly on the ground! His extraordinary skills have attracted the attention of university scientists researching psychic phenomena, and countless numbers of journalists and documentary producers.

Notes

Notes

Notes

We hope you enjoyed this Hay House book.
If you'd like to receive a free catalog featuring additional
Hay House books and products, or if you'd like information
about the Hay Foundation, please contact:

Hay House, Inc.
P.O. Box 5100
Carlsbad, CA 92018-5100

**(760) 431-7695 or (800) 654-5126
(760) 431-6948 (fax) or (800) 650-5115 (fax)
www.hayhouse.com**

❈ ❈ ❈

Published and distributed in Australia by:
Hay House Australia Pty. Ltd. • 18/36 Ralph St. • Alexandria NSW 2015 •
Phone: 612-9669-4299 • *Fax:* 612-9669-4144 • www.hayhouse.com.au

Published and distributed in the United Kingdom by:
Hay House UK, Ltd. • Unit 62, Canalot Studios •
222 Kensal Rd., London W10 5BN • *Phone:* 44-20-8962-1230 •
Fax: 44-20-8962-1239 • www.hayhouse.co.uk

Published and distributed in the Republic of South Africa by:
Hay House SA (Pty), Ltd., P.O. Box 990, Witkoppen 2068 •
Phone/Fax: 27-11-706-6612 • orders@psdprom.co.za

Distributed in Canada by:
Raincoast • 9050 Shaughnessy St., Vancouver, B.C. V6P 6E5 •
Phone: (604) 323-7100 • *Fax:* (604) 323-2600

❈ ❈ ❈

Tune in to **www.hayhouseradio.com**™ for the best in inspirational talk
radio featuring top Hay House authors! And, sign up via the Hay House
USA Website to receive the Hay House online newsletter and stay
informed about what's going on with your favorite authors. You'll
receive bimonthly announcements about: Discounts and Offers, Special
Events, Product Highlights, Free Excerpts, Giveaways, and more!
www.hayhouse.com